The Place

What you have been seeking that you always knew was possible

Gary M. Douglas

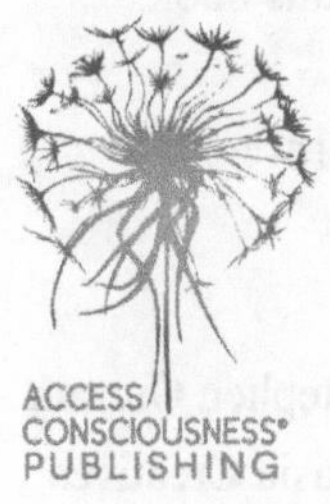

The Place

ACCESS CONSCIOUSNESS PUBLISHING COMPANY, LLC
Santa Barbara, California
www.AccessConsciousnessPublishing.com

Second Edition 2013
Printed in the United States of America
International printing in the U.K. and Australia
First Edition by Big Country Publishing 2011

ISBN-13: 978-1-939261-14-4
ISBN-10: 1939261147

Cover Photography by: Stephen Outram
Interior Design by: Anastasia Creatives

Acknowledgements

Dona Haber - a remarkable editor who gets what I am really doing.

Special thanks to Dain Heer, Simone Milasas, Nancy O'Conner, Wendy Hart and Vanitha Subramthian.

Thanks to Stephen Outram who has created an amazing website and a book cover that speaks, and is a man who contributes in ways he doesn't even know!

Special thanks to all the women in my past who educated me on what could be, what should be and what doesn't exist.

Chapter One

As I drove through the pines, the wind whistling around me, the roar of the engine of my '57 thunderbird was a sweet reminder of the times past when life was slower and technology not the source of life.

After two hours I had seen no cars on this back road leading to Idaho. Why Idaho? I don't know anymore, it was just the memory of so many years in the past, the quiet, the tranquility, the pines, the silent streams and that one time when I stopped at the crossroads to nowhere and the only sounds were the lilt of the soft wind in the trees and a single bird and the pop of the engine. One of those profound moments when your soul soars, your mind opens and the intensity of space reflects some inner peace that escapes you when you go back to the world of planes, trains, cars and incessant clatter.

The years since had been filled with all that is considered right in life. The marriage—the beautiful dark-haired, funny, laughing girl who disappeared during the long nights of normal—those insane attempts to be like others that suffocate the being and mold us into the humiliated wrongness of never truly fitting but always trying so very hard to be normal.

The child—sweet promise that the world will be better because he, like Jesus, will save the world, or at least ours. What a burden to place on those small soft shoulders. The smiles heal; the joy of life lessens the agony and monotony of sameness as the jobs of life smother your own joys.

The divorce—what we love in each other dies in each day as we force ourselves to fit in the box of indistinct work, self-blinding carnage of the "true world, real world, real life" and the dreams, the possibilities and the joys drift to a past that others call unreal, stupid, insane, hopeless and just plain wrong.

Now I drive, the forest and the streams and the wind blessing me with their energy and their lack of judgment, embracing me with the gifts of shade, smell, light and sparkling contentment with life.

I pull off the road behind some scrubby willows where others have obviously stopped before me, the trash of their passing a testament to the bizarre lack of caring and the foolish disregard for beauty and silence. Probably these are those same great people who go camping in the woods, taking their culture of boom box and beer to the frontier of silence to dissipate the space and create the confines of awareness and make the lacks of life bearable.

I sit in the car, have I mentioned that I left the top at home? The weather will dictate my rest. As I sit, the silence begins to soothe my weary soul and my body in a way I have not experienced since last I came this way. I open the door and slide out of the car, in front of me is a lazy stream and sandy beach, I slide out of my clothes and walk slowly into the water. It is chilly even this late in the summer. The goose pimples tell me I am still alive; I walk towards the rock submerged a couple of feet below the surface. As I sit, the cold water on my crotch makes me stumble and I fall into the water. I come up with the same joy my little boy does when he plays in the surf or the pool. I suddenly miss his smile, his kisses, and the "Daddy, I love you so much" that precedes hugs and requests for toys. I sit on the rock and tears stream down my face.

As the silence and peace of the stream embrace me and my body with a sense of finally belonging somewhere, somehow, someway, the tension begins to dissipate and the tiny fish begin to nibble on the hairs of my body as though these will bring their next meal. For me, it is the sensation that I have shut off so that I don't have to feel the gnawing knowledge that I should be able to revel in the innate sensorial perversity that bodies enjoy. The tears that drop salt into this sweet stream, that, like true life, meanders in the easiest and blessed way that none live in the clattering world of choice-less menu, that menu that has too many choices, so that we can make no choice as real, and as life. Suddenly the stupidity of no choice gives way to the burst of laughter that creates the awareness of the oneness that I, too, belong with nature and am part of the stream of life and that it and I are the same. I have always felt separate and alone and finally I know I belong and that the pain I have lived as greater than me is truly the insane stupidity of making that greater than me in order to truly believe I have no choice.

What now? I sit in this wonderful place and rest, allowing the past to leach out into the water. Silently around the corner of the stream, a beautiful mallard woman sails down the stream, her cute ducklings following, silent bullets of sweet life that feel close to me. I sit with my space larger than I have ever known was possible and these sweet creatures see me as non-threatening. Apparently the smell of me is no longer a wrongness, and they come towards me; the little ones see me with curiosity and come close to find out what I am. My hands floating with the stream suddenly look like somewhere to land and the little duck who is most aggressive lands upon my hand, his little claws digging in for safety. The tiny pain is as nothing compared with the pain I have made greater than my choice of life. Laughter bursts forth from a place I didn't even know existed, a place without the ability to separate or judge where I begin and the others end.

The mother duck flies, and the babies, without the feathers to follow, flap brilliantly and fumble greatly in the need to flee this strange being who in joy makes way too much noise.

After they have gone, I lift my body from the sweet coolness that somehow allows everything to seem better and begin to walk towards my car.

The succulent sun and the caressing breeze begin to dry my body. I pull on my pants, which suddenly feel too tight after the freedom and joy of flowing with and as the stream; I pull on my t-shirt, suddenly aware of the feel of muscles that desire to be caressed again for the first time in seven years.

I climb into the car and start it, enjoying again the rumble of this sweet old beauty that is always a gift of exuberance and fun that only driving has given me before today. The real gift of today is somehow finding the me I knew ought to exist but has not.

Back on the road, I race through the dappled light of the failing sun, realizing the sounds of the birds I had filtered out of my awareness before the stream and recognizing the breeze and the wind and the smells of the trees are now accompanied by the intensity of the dryness of summer and the subtle underlying compost of dropping leaves and aromatic earth, speaking of how I belong.

As the sun disappears amongst the tall and elegant trees and the temperature begins to ease, I think of the soft jazz music that once was the source of such kindness to my soul, and I reach over to the glove box that is the hiding spot for the top-of-the line stereo I had installed just to piss my wife off and pull out CDs that will match the mood I'm sure is the new beginning for my life. I drive as the soft cloak of darkness descends upon me and the headlights become the total of space and time. Minutes turn to hours and still I drive.

Occasionally another car passes, a momentary flash of a bigger picture, a reminiscent flash of the day not finished but experienced.

The CD completes on one of those soft plaintive notes, as though I, too, have reached some unknown completion. I reach for another CD and drop it on the floor—aw shit, I hate when I do that—I reach over to the floor of the passenger side seeking what I cannot see, find it and sit up. There in front of me is a five-point buck dead in the headlights, frozen.

I swerve to miss him, and there is nothing but large boulders in front of the car and no place to go, I jam the brakes, the car is sliding in the gravel next to the edge and then I hit the edge and slide into the boulders and the screech of tearing metal and the crunch of the door next to me change into the loft of the car, and my body as it rips into the darkness and I land on my back against hard and vicious nature, my breath expelled with the force of blackness that wraps my mind away from what I cannot stand to feel.

With a shriek of pain, I am suddenly aware of the semi-light that glares at me. It is the one remaining headlight of my mangled beauty, the car that was the last hope and promise of something better. I croak a feeble call for help. The only answer is the cessation of crickets and nighttime insects and the faint hoot of a far-off owl. Time to take stock. Okay, I've been unconscious. My car is off the road. There is only one light and that's looking pretty dim so maybe I've been out a long time. The road is above me so if anyone passes will they see me? I'm on my back, what can I move? My left arm is free and the hand moves, the right seems to be stuck against something and is asleep but it hurts, I try to move it, and as it slips from underneath my body the pain increases and the blackness enfolds me once again.

I open my eyes and the light from the headlight is dimmer yet, how long does it take for a battery to wear down, how long has it been? I gave up watches when my life fell apart. I reach out with my right hand and there just past the elbow is a small sapling about three inches thick. If I can reach that with my left hand, maybe I can pull myself up the embankment to the road. I reach over with my left, the pain almost unbearable, but I've decided, no more passing out, so I don't. I grab the tree and pulling with all my might my body begins to turn, and so does lights out, so much for decision.

I awaken again, the light from the car is now just the filament looking warm and weak. Well, at least I'm face down, even with a mouth full of gravel, and suddenly I realize it has been a long time since I've eaten. I reach up with both hands looking for something to pull myself up the bank. A small bush by the right hand. I grab and pull and the bush rips loose from the embankment. The left hand checks—and nothing. All right, dig in with both hands and pull, the dirt gives way and my body goes nowhere. Please, someone find me, please God, let someone come. Amazing how religious I can be at a time of helplessness.

Time to try pushing with the legs, I pull the right leg slowly up, or at least so says the brain, but nothing happens. Please let someone come to help. I try again and pull with my hands, dig in with the toes and push, blackness envelops me in her sweet arms again.

I feel a sweet small hand, is it illusion or is my son trying to awaken me from some bad dream? "Mister, do you need help?" This small voice is matched on the other side of me with a duplicate sound… "Mister, would you like us to help you?"

"Where did you kids come from?"

"The place, where everything is possible."

"Please can you go for help?"

"Sure, mister." They reply in unison as though they are the same voice in stereo from different sides of my head.

"Do you want to go?" says the right. "Why don't you go?" says the left. "You know we both better go," says the right. "Oh, yeah, 'cause you know what they will need" says the left. "Oh, Yeah," says the right. A small hand descends toward my third eye and the sweet voice of this child says, "You sleep now, mister, we'll be back with our sister and uncle, just sleep, just sleep," and suddenly as if by magic I am once again the victim of blackness.

I awaken once again, the early morning ground mist filters the light, I am on my back. I look up into the most beautiful blue eyes attached to a radiant face kissed by the sun and blessed by the gods of old. Her smile and her complete lack of concern are somehow very comforting. "Who are you?" I ask.

"My name is Ruth, like in the Bible." The accent is somehow strange and familiar all at once. She is dressed in one of those hippie-looking dresses you used to see in the sixties, long, tight on top and falling from below the breasts. As she moves around me the material draping from side to side, the possibility of a great body seems to haunt some strange memory.

I hear the sounds of feet moving through gravel and a big bear of a man leans over me, his breath reminiscent of the sweet grain that is fed to horses.

"Well, young fella, you ain't in the best of shapes. How'd you end up here in this mess in the middle of nowhere?"

I start to remember what happened, the music, the CD, and then the deer and the shriek of metal and trying to move, and what do I say? Where do I start? And then I think of my life and the creek and the ducks, and....

"Well that's a lot to take in, in such a short time, but we're gonna have to move you now, and that might be a little painful, so...." And his big calloused hand descends towards my third eye and blackness once again embraces me.

Chapter Two

The sunlight filters through the crack in the curtains taking away the longing for sleep in favor of the craving for the out-of-doors and air that will caress my body. Boy, a run would be great about now… and then with a flash, the whole accident comes rushing back and the questions begin. I look around the room. It is clean and bright and reminds me of my grandfather's farmhouse. His house had begun as a log cabin, one big room that had been added to over the years until it was more Victorian than farm. This still has the feel of that one room beginning, definitely log and not new, unlike those kit homes, this one has different sized logs hand hewn to make the sides symmetrical.

The old Victorian furniture appears to be like 1860s and the bed is really small, like maybe a full size. The curtains at the window are that gingham print that no one uses, a cliché for the olden days. Maybe this place is some kind of dude ranch or camp from yesteryear. I've heard of those, just never been near one. I look around for the TV that every good place has, but there isn't one. Maybe that only exists at the lodge. Phone, maybe there's a phone. But who would I call? My ex would just ask why I bothered to survive, and I wouldn't want to worry my son. I guess it's not relevant. I look down at my legs, which hadn't worked very well a few hours ago—or was it days or weeks ago? I suddenly realize that time stopped when I saw that deer and I have no idea when, where or how I am.

The door swings open, its ancient looking hinges only squeaking slightly as she enters the room. The tray of steaming something attracts my attention like a homing beacon for hungry baby birds, my salivation kicks into high gear.

"Hello, do I remember correctly, your name is Ruth?"

"Yes, Jacob Rayne, you are correct." Odd, I don't remember telling her my name, but I guess she would have gotten that from my driver's license.

"I seem to be rather hungry, how long have I been here?"

"You've been here seven days now, mostly healing and mostly not choosing to be awake and conscious. That occurs with rather severe injuries, don't worry." How the hell did she know I was worrying? Something is truly weird here.

I looked at the beautiful face surrounded by that soft golden hair and as she moved towards me, I became intensely aware of that same serene presence that had created such calm at the accident.

"Where am I? Has the doctor been here? How badly am I hurt?"

She smiled at me with the elegance of a movie queen of the 1940s and the sweetness of a shy virgin from the south and merely sat on the bed next to me.

"I believe you have enough strength in your arms to slide up so that you can eat more easily." Once again that haunting accent that was both familiar and strange, I wondered where she was from. "Don't use your legs, they're not strong yet and it will probably hurt a great deal."

I pushed myself into a reclining position like some slightly retarded teen, and she reached behind me and fluffed the pillows so that I was no longer flat on my back.

"Please, may I feed you, it's only oats, with a little milk and sugar, but Uncle Jed said that would be all your stomach would tolerate today. There's been no doctor, this is just a small mountain village and we sort of lost touch with the outside world a while back. We just live on our own and stay out of the clatter of modern life. Uncle Jed says the breaks in your legs should heal fine and that the damage to your spine will take a little time, but he doesn't see any reason why you won't be a hundred percent by the time the snow comes."

I have an odd feeling that I really should be asking some questions or demanding some answers, but that serene countenance and lack of any concern, once again requires nothing but acceptance.

"What about my car? Is she still at the road?"

"Oh, the twins brought your car here and they're having a great time trying to heal her. We've never had a thing like her before, so they're not really sure what to do for her. Why do you call her, her?"

As she spooned the sweet, gritty oats into my mouth, I tried to think back and I couldn't remember talking about my car. I had only called her "her" a couple of times before my wife made fun of me for being so stupid and after that I only thought of her as "her." Maybe in my delirium, if I had any, I'd said something.

"You were never delirious, just unconscious or asleep, so you don't have to consider fevers or those kinds of problems."

Well, that's at least one answer, though God knows, I can't bring that into context so that it fits what I know. Weird, this is sort of like being in that Kathy Bates and James Caan movie where she keeps that guy captive and never really gives a straight answer so that he will stay with her. Have I stumbled on some strange cult that captures and keeps unsuspecting strangers? I'm getting as paranoid as I was when I was married, expecting the worst and then getting it.

Try again. "So did the doctor come when I was unconscious, is that how you know what's wrong with my legs and spine, and is there some reason why you don't answer my questions?"

"Jacob, there are some questions that are not mine to answer, so they must wait for those who can, I recognize how frustrating this seems, but I cannot give you what I cannot explain."

As she completes her speech, the door hinges announce the arrival of a new visitor and I look up into the grizzled bearded face of the man who put me to sleep back at the road.

"Hello there, Jacob, I'm Jedidiah Ramsey, the head of our clan, and I am the one who must explain to you the things that are not normal about us here."

As he begins to speak, Ruth slips silently out of the room without even saying goodbye, gliding across the floor like a sylph of old, pausing to look at me as she closes the door behind her. A longing for her sweet face and for her kind presence swells in my chest, and I think I cannot handle the intensity of feelings I have suppressed and hidden for years in order to cope with all that does not work in life. I feel what I can only describe as a kiss upon my being that somehow I know comes from her. This is the romantic man's fantasy come true, one who touches your soul even when not present. Can this be real, is she real, have I found that which I believed ought to exist, but never found is true and real, here in this odd place? Whoa, I just went from paranoia straight to belief in what is only imagination in less than an hour, well I may not be delirious, but I've got a strong stranglehold on delusion.

Uncle Jed lets out a deep breath and opens his mouth, and I anticipate something and am acutely aware of the confusion that marches across the fine features of a man who is both old and ageless. Each time I have looked at him, I have seen the elements that one calls age, but now as I look closely, I see crow's-feet where there should be lines, and vibrant skin where there should be sags, and even though the beard could hide some of that, I look at these two brown eyes that are clear and bright and simultaneously speak of experience that brings wisdom and pain that brings tolerance and time that allows peace. Those eyes are a window to the peace that only comes to long life, a life of knowing that the choices others must make and the struggles they choose cannot be changed, but with awareness they will open to the gifts of the possibilities that exist. My grandfather had been one of those men who could see that people will choose that which should not be chosen and speak that which should never be spoken, and after many years the disappointment over that which will never be chosen, and the nurturance and goodness that kindness gifts to those who stay when others quit, and the depth of caring that only great gulps of life imbibe, which leave a fathomless look of what can best be described as the embodiment of indefinite life, seeing that which is greater, that which could be, and never mourning for that which will not be. I know I can trust this man.

"Well, then Jacob, thanks for the trust, I will do my best to honor that, and I will answer all your questions to the best of my ability. I only ask that you give me time to find the way to explain to you some things I don't fully understand myself."

"First of all, we aren't a cult, but we do have some differences that make us stay away from the rest of the world. We have been here in this place for a long time and being isolated from the rest of the world, we had to develop certain, I guess you'd call them talents in order to handle the different things that show up in life. I developed what you might call healing abilities; I'm sort of the doctor for our group. I began years ago to be able to feel the difference in the spots in the body when somebody broke an arm or a leg, and after a while I started seeing exactly what it looked like, and then I could talk to the body and begin its repair. You know the morning the boys brought us to you when I touched you and you went to sleep, well, that thars, what I learned to do, to take away pain. It sort of short circuits the response systems of the brain and brings relaxation. I never ran into a spine problem like yours before, but I believe that your body wants to be well and it will repair with a little time. So what else would you like to know?"

Is this really happening? I don't understand how I could trust so easily after years of training myself to be a skeptic and more years living in a relationship that started great and slowly became a brainwashing to produce the man I didn't know and wanted not to be. What is the matter with me? I am acting as though all this is normal and I don't need to worry anymore. What do I mean anymore?

I'm thinking thoughts that shouldn't be thought, about people I don't know and accepting things that are said as though I have functioned like this forever.

"Am I on some kind of drugs? Where am I really and what do you people want of me?" That's better, sounding a little more annoyed and paranoid seems like me. "And by the way, who are those kids who found me and what were they doing out on the road in the middle of the night?"

The laughter that exudes from Uncle Jed like the musical notes of amorous teenage boys strikes me like a splash of cold water.

"No, boy, we haven't drugged you, and you happen to be about forty miles from the road where you got hurt, and it's hard to hold on to skepticism and paranoia when people just care. We stay away from the rest of the world for many reasons but mostly because those in your world believe that distrust makes them safe; we are safe because we believe in what we do and what we are. I guess you would say we have trust in ourselves. When you have trust in yourself, those that don't have trust in themselves have a hard time holding onto their distrust. I believe that you will recognize that difference with us. The boys are Ruth's nephews. Their father left before they were born and their mother died giving birth."

"But I thought you were a healer, why couldn't you save her?" My thoughtless question, not really a question but a reproach and a dedication to my own lack of trust, sent the old man into aging decades in seconds. The lines appeared and the sags were obvious and then suddenly gone.

"I am a healer, Jacob, but when someone you love loses the will to live, no matter what you would wish, you cannot heal them. She was my child and I wanted more for her than she did. Not even the promise of sweet boy children would change her mind. Choice is ours to use as we wish."

"Can I call you Uncle Jed or would that be disrespectful?"

"Yes, Jacob, you can call me Uncle Jed. I would be honored."

"Would you like to officially meet the boys?"

"Yes, please, I need to thank them for finding me."

"Okay boys, you can come in now," and the door began to creep open and there stood two look-a-like boys about twelve years old, their bright blue eyes seeming to take up the whole of my vision, like being a bug under a magnifying glass. The effect was instant and somewhat disconcerting, usually little kids don't leave me with the feeling that I am naked to the soul, but these two did.

Uncle Jed coughed, and that strange feeling left and the boys smiled with a sweetness and joyfulness that left me feeling as though some odd conversation had occurred without my hearing anything.

"Hi, my name is Rob," said number one, and number two said, "and I'm Roy," and both said simultaneously, "You was sure messed up mister when we found you, but you're looking a lot better now, Uncle Jed is cool, and Ruth can create some good stuff too, she fixed your face, it was kind of crooked that first night. Would you tell us about 'her' we never had one of 'her' kind here and we ain't sure what to do next."

I was really confused, what 'her' are these kids talking about. And then suddenly I remembered what Ruth had said about my car.

"That's my car, she was sort of my pride and joy. I sure hope she can be repaired and made to look good again."

The boys looked at each other with a flicker of laughter teasing the corners of their mouths, and once again that strange feeling of being peeled naked came over me, and I could feel a flood of memories of the car and what she looked like surfacing like memories from the past that get triggered by tastes and smells or music and touch, viscerally complete and full of texture.

Uncle Jed did that throat clearing thing and the intensity of memory disappeared. "Okay boys, you got the information you needed, now it's time to answer that man's questions."

Rob spoke first, "Mister Rayne, me and Roy heard you a lot of years ago, we have the ability to hear those that desire the future they believe ought to exist and we can hear that longing and need. We also hear when you call for help. The night you got hurt, we could hear you calling. When someone calls to us with great need, we will arrive in minutes, just like we did with you."

"What do you mean, you can arrive in minutes?" That strange feeling of sliding sideways began, and I was certain that what was real did not include what my mind had just surmised as truth... it couldn't be true. Uncle Jed's hand reaches for my forehead and I knew that the sweet darkness that required no question was approaching and it descended.

Chapter Three

The morning stole into my awareness with that roll of the drum like thunder in the distance and the buzz of the insects and the sweet nectar song of the birds. Why is it that birds are totally joyful at the beginning of each day and we humans moan and rail against the sun rising and beg for more darkness? Are we just dedicated to misery and some strange belief that bed is the one place of safety from one another that will grant us the peace we so strikingly avoid as though we will be infected like the birds with the ultimate stupidity called happiness?

The hunger gnawing at the door of response is answered with the creak of the door hinges, why don't they grease those things, and Ruth bursts into the room with her serenity and ease, a smile and a tray that my nose screams is bacon and eggs. I pull myself up, conscious of the need to leave my legs alone and she leans over to fluff my pillows and my recently not alive body begins to have signs of life from the smell of that beautiful hair and the kindness I never knew actually existed in a woman but always prayed for. As she pulls away from me I can't believe my eyes, but she is blushing.

"We don't grease the hinges so that you will always know that we are coming."

Oh God, she can read my mind, now I'm embarrassed, 'cause now I know why she blushed and what else have I thought that I'd rather she not know about me, except if someone can read your mind, can you really keep secrets? How the hell does relationship work here? That's a degree of intimacy I doubt I could live with.

"Jacob, maybe by now, you realize that we are a little different. We communicate telepathically, as you would call it, and we allow ourselves to know what is coming before it arrives most times. We could not know about your accident, but we did know you were coming."

I feel like I've been slammed by a locomotive, my breath is short, and I close my eyes and begin to shake my head. This can't be true, I've lost my mind. I open my mouth and my eyes to respond, and the twins are standing beside my bed, one on each side, those shiny laughing eyes attesting to the devilment they are enjoying, and I suspect it's at my expense. Did I just pass out for a moment or did they hide under the bed and pop up while I was contemplating all this?

"No Jacob, we weren't under the bed, we just did what we did the night you got hurt." Which is it—Rob or Roy—how do I tell these two apart, they look too much alike. "I'm Roy, here take my hand and then you will be able to feel the difference in us the way we know you and the difference you are for us, it's how we know who's thinking what and where." I take his sweet hand, boy, do I miss my son, those soft hands make me think of him. "It's not that you are thinking of your son, your son and I have a similar vibration, we would be good friends." "Now hold my hand," says Rob. As I take his hands, the sense is that the baby ducks are on my body. Together, "Okay now Mister Rayne, close your eyes and feel the difference."

As I close my eyes, they release my hands and suddenly I feel the ducks in the right hand and the son energy in the left hand. I open my eyes and I can't tell the difference. "Close your eyes." I do and there is once again the change from side to side of that odd feeling. I open my eyes and look, and the boys are gone. I blink and shake my head and again they are there by the bed. One of the boys takes my hand and I feel the energy of my son and the intense need I don't want to know I have of him, "You're Roy, right?" "Yes, sir." Then I close my eyes and put my attention on the left and I feel the energy switch several times and I open my eyes and look at the boy on my right and I feel the baby ducks… "Oh, my god, I know which is which, you're Rob!"

The fact that I now can shut my eyes and feel the difference between these two seems astounding, but I do remember being in bed with more than two people and always knowing who I was touching. I guess it really isn't strange; I just want it to be so, so I can believe everything I am experiencing is either terribly right or terribly wrong, the operative word being terribly.

The smiles on the two boys' faces radiate a joy that I have missed in the young friends of my son's who always are grateful when us old people actually get the brilliance and brightness that innately exudes from small bodies. I feel like I have climbed Mount Everest for them and as though there is some wall that has disintegrated and I am acutely aware of everything. I recognize the vibration of Ruth, and, as I do, tears begin to run down my face. This is the woman I have been dreaming of for ten years, no wonder the voice is haunting, I've heard it at least twice a week for years and the smell of her hair and light in the window and joy in my heart for finally knowing that who and what I wanted actually exists, and the memory of the sex that I had in dreams begins to make my blood sing, and my heart pounds and my body breathes deeply of the life it has always searched for and only vaguely believed could truly exist, bursting like a balloon that is overfilled and seeps the joy of living into the pores of my body, in a way that no one has ever told me about or demonstrated yet seems both right and greater than anything I ever conceived possible. My senses extending around the room feel vaguely that there is a wrinkle in the universe like they talked about in Star Wars, and I look at Ruth, who is crying too. She knows, or knew, or suspected or experienced the same thing I did, how can this be?

The boys speak together. “Mr. Rayne, we all perceived the place where you and Ruth live with one another. Here we know everything, and nothing is a wrongness. We like that you make each other happy. You asked for us years ago when you came this way and you have been part of us ever since.”

I want to be embarrassed by the fact that these boys have been privy to my private universe, but instead I am at peace. As they continue to talk to me I notice that although I hear them, their lips are not moving. Am I losing my mind, am I delusional or is this a dream and I will awaken soon?

“No Jacob, this is not a dream, this is the way of true communication, the boys and Uncle Jed and the rest of us have a direct line to one another. You’ve always had this and you thought it was serendipity when you knew what others were thinking or when to call them or when you had a glimpse of the future. For us this is normal; you call it psychic.”

As Ruth finished her explanation, I knew that everything I had experienced with these people was so normal that I felt at home for the first time in my life. I truly belonged somewhere... here.

The boys vanish from the room as Ruth moves towards me. My ailing body suddenly springs to life with a vitality it knew when it was nineteen, that first time.

As she arrives next to me, not embarrassed at all, she bends and her dress disappears, just like in my dreams, and I wonder how it will be in person. Oh God, don't let me die of extreme bliss. She reaches out and touches my hand and as she kisses me, energy erupts in every cell of my body and darkness descends, gloriously, graciously, with an expansiveness of life I have never felt.

Chapter Four

I awaken to the exuberance of the birds, the intensity of the breeze in the pines and extended sense of someone coming. No, not someone, Ruth. I stretch, arching my back and pushing my legs toward the end of the bed. Whoa, it didn't hurt, how can that be, yesterday I couldn't even move them. The hinges squeak and she enters, my breakfast, my nose says fruit and something warm that I don't recognize and the feast for my eyes, her.

She smiles. "Jake, sex is a form of healing, an energy that invites the body back to the memory of itself, but when it is that, your body needs sleep, not physical accomplishment."

"So, why are you speaking this morning, instead of giving it to me just with your mind?"

"Learning to hear with just your mind takes time unless the twins are here. What they do is bend space. It's what you do when you drive somewhere and get there sooner than you should. When you bend space, you can appear and disappear the way the boys do, but you also change the space so the person you are with experiences the loss of time and matter as the source of life and moves to a level of being that expands and generates different possibilities."

"Wow, thanks," I think. "I feel like I just got a lesson in quantum physics, on my first day of kindergarten. Is there any way you can explain that to stupid people, 'cause apparently, today, I'm stupid."

"I'll try. Time is not real, it's a construct that the world uses to justify not embodying every awareness and communication with molecular structure that would allow for destruction to be an unnecessary part of life."

"Well that was certainly clearer."

Her laughter tickles the small hairs on my arms, and the sarcastic remark obviously created the result I was looking for. "So, if that sex healed me this much, how about a little more to improve the ol' bod?"

Once again the laughter tickles my hair, what a fabulous thing it is to feel such extreme desire and at the same time, absolutely no need for that sexual energy which I always thought had to lead to dark and bed.

"Well, Mr. Rayne, you can only awaken the body a little at a time without changing its structure in ways you might find discomforting, besides, if we save something for later, you will get far more out of it."

The look in her eye is sexier and more stirring than any I have ever seen before and I know that this is not just a tease, but a promise I can count on to come to orgasm. The smile on my face at my own pun initiates another tickling laughter just as the hinges signal a new arrival and my senses tell me it's Uncle Jed.

"Good morning, Jacob, eat your breakfast, the feast for the eyes is leaving now." With that wonderful floating elegance, Ruth smiles as she meanders from the room leaving me breathless and excited simultaneously.

I look at the breakfast in front of me, the berries pungent with sweetness, and the aroma of the strange meat on the plate is succulent with smoke and tangles of flavors I have never had. "Looks and smells good." As my fork cuts the delicate meat, the aroma of wild tangles amongst my taste buds and lingers like a haunting phrase in a great play. "What is this, Uncle Jed?"

"Jacob, that thar is a rattlesnake that crawled in here the other night to be a gift to us and our bodies. You recall the way I said we was different, well we call to the critters who are willing to gift their bodies for the sustenance of ours. Ruth, me, the boys and the others who have been here a while, don't really need much to eat, but as you have to recover there are certain meats, berries, and vegetables as well as certain herbs, that your body tells us it needs energetically to get itself healthy. So we call and they come and show themselves to us."

The rattlesnake tastes so good I can't stop eating it, even though I would like so much to be repulsed by the idea that I'm eating snake. Sensing the truth that the snake had come of its own volition somehow makes it taste even better.

"Uncle Jed, how did this place come to be and how did you get here and what does it mean that I asked for you and this place?"

"Well, son, that thar's a lot of questions all of which require a lengthy explanation. How about I do a little healing on your body and try to give you the best answer I can, 'cause I don't actually have all the pieces to that puzzle at my fingertips, but I promise I'll do my best. Just close your eyes and let me tell you a story of how we found 'the place'."

Chapter Five

"Back in 1860, our families decided to leave the Georgia woods we had lived in so very long, nigh on fifty years. Of course, our family had been a little wealthier than our neighbors, so we got just a bit high-and-mighty and seriously invested our money in things we didn't know about. When the Great Depression of 1830 hit, we lost most everything, most of our land and all of our slaves. We managed to retain about a 160 acres of bottom land and the house, but it warn't enough to take care of the twenty odd relatives, brothers, sisters and cousins. When the south began to talk of secession, we all voted and decided to leave, there wasn't much except more of not enough and the rumbling of war on the horizon. So the whole danged family started praying for a 'place' where we could find the best that life could offer. A few months after our prayers, a neighbor offered to buy us out, and we took the money, got wagons, horses, cows, pigs, sheep, ducks and chickens and formed our wagon train to head west. It was still winter when we left, and it was hard getting to Kansas City, which is where a whole passel of wagon trains headed west. Most went for the Dakotas, but we wanted to go to Oregon. God knows how we came to choose Oregon, when most folks was heading elsewhere.

Well, we had two months before the spring thaws would make travel easy, and as some of the family got jobs and others were spirited away for brides, our numbers diminished. We put out that we was a religious group that wanted a leader who could take us to Oregon.

About a month before we was to leave, a man came, he was dirty, old, and missin' three fingers on his right hand. He said he was a God-fearing man, who was married to an Indian squaw and could take us to Oregon. The fifteen of us that were left voted, and since we had not met any other scouts that would take us, mostly because we didn't have a lot of money to pay, we decided to go. About a week later we packed up our five wagons, all the animals and all the furniture we had left and set out for Oregon."

Chapter Six

"The details of the trip have long since faded from memory. Suffice it to say that we had encounters with Indians, but never seemed to have any trouble from them. Our scout, John MacDonald, Mac for short, always left with his wife to parlay with them and always came back with a request for a sheep or a cow or some salt or sugar, but not anything else. His wife—we all called her Mrs. Mac 'cause none of us could pronounce her name—was a silent woman who had the oddest habit of showing up all the time with whatever you was in need of and she didn't apparently speak any English.

After about four months of travel, everything started to go wrong. Wheels that were supposed to be new rotted. The salt pork that was a staple of our diet went bad. We started hunting more, but failed to see or catch much as it had been a drought time and there wasn't much game on this trail.

Mr. Mac came down with a fever after cutting his hand on one of the rusty tools we had brought but not taken care of, and no one knew what to do for him. His wife sat beside him and would touch his forehead periodically and he would sleep. She would sing to him those chanting songs Indians use and the strange peace that prevailed left us all feeling better, like everything would be all right.

After twenty days of the fever, Mr. Mac died. We buried him there and in our distraught moments, realized we had no idea what to do. We gathered together and prayed for help, took out the compass and decided which way was west. We got the remaining four wagons together—we had already cannibalized one in order to take care of broken pieces—and headed out.

Mrs. Mac went with us, and as we were not any longer total green horns, at least in our own minds, we tried to pick our way through canyons and hills. Every once in a while she would point to some direction we had thought was all wrong, yet always turned out to be easier than what we chose.

After another three weeks of travel, the weather began to turn, fall fell upon us with thunder, lightning and rains the likes of which we had never seen. The creeks that we had been fording with ease began to become rivers and what had been easy began to be very hard.

Matilda Ramsey, the mother of John and Jed, had gotten pregnant a short time before we left and the child decided that this was a good time to come. We held up the progress of our train two weeks so that Stormy—that's what we called the baby—could come. It seemed like an odd name, but every time we mentioned how stormy it was, she would stop fussin' so we figured she was telling us something, and every time we called her Ellen, the name first chosen, she would wail to beat the band.

With light snow falling, we set out agin, thinking that we couldn't be far from civilization, we'd been on the road so long, we must find people soon. Mrs. Mac pointed in a direction that wasn't quite west, but she had been so much better at picking spots that we chose to follow her lead. It was actually sort of strange, the way she had, without force or vote or talk, become the one we trusted and followed."

Chapter Seven

"About four days after starting again, we came to a river that boiled and rolled and roared like an untamed beast. We looked for the calmest part so we could cross and found it about a mile down river, a place that was quiet and calm looking and not too deep. Mrs. Mac kept pointing up river, but all we saw there was more rapid and difficult looking, so we chose our point for entry, not hers.

As we began to cross the river, the first wagon in was Matilda's, she and the children and her husband Joseph. About two thirds of the way through, the wagon stopped moving, the horses began to rear and scream, and the current started to turn them sideways. The horses began to be dragged backwards towards the rapids that were just beyond the quiet area and the family started to scream, too. Mrs. Mac and several of the men moved their horses into the river, which, without warning, had suddenly risen two feet and with their animals bucking the tide, they raced against what seemed the inevitable.

The wagon trembled as it hit a rock not far from the bank and began to break apart. Those on the shore watched with horror as the family fell one by one into the roaring waters and were swallowed up. Mrs. Mac somehow got to what was left of the wagon and grabbed Stormy and Jed and held the baby in her arms and managed to keep Jed behind her and still managed to get her horse to swim back to the rest of us.

None of the men had been able to save the others. Our group sat on the bank of the river, mourning not only the loss of family, but also the food, stock and animals that had been in the wagon and those wonderful horses that had taken such great care of us in the past months of travel and hardships.

Mrs. Mac jumped from her horse, Stormy in her arms, quiet and sweet like no one had ever seen her before. Jed sat there freezing and wet and crying. Mrs. Mac began gathering firewood and started a fire. The rest of the group suddenly came to life. They gathered blankets for Jed and Stormy, Ulah May gathered Stormy to her and let Mrs. Mac move freely and Lulah May, her sister, threw blankets around Mrs. Mac, who somehow was now not only the savior, but also family. Only family risks their lives for you, or the greatest of friends, either way she had now become ours as she had made us hers. Indian, silent, no English, none of that meant anything anymore. Gratitude for what she had done overrode even the sadness of losing family. Gratitude for one who risked and saved—she would never be forgotten."

Chapter Eight

"Days later after finding two of the bodies and burying them, we started north for the place that Mrs. Mac had tried to show us before. Apparently, there had been storms in the mountains before us that had brought the river to a greater height.

Now we all reeked of fear at the prospect of going across the river, but we had not enough food and it was too far back to people, so we sat and watched, hoping against hope that the river would fall. Mrs. Mac sat waiting and then went to her horse and swung up, she walked over to Ulah May, who handed her the baby and she headed for the river. As she entered the rapidly moving water, everyone cried out 'No.' She stopped and looked back at us and then rode on. The panic that everyone felt was palpable and the recent loss of so many to this same river left each of us with the certainty that disaster was imminent. In the middle of the river, the horse began to rise out of the water and within a few feet it was only ankle deep in water and we finally understood what we had missed about this area before. Apparently, the water had overrun the bank and was actually shallower here than anywhere else. We all knew we would never doubt Mrs. Mac again. Within minutes we had harnessed up and were following Mrs. Mac, who waited on the other side of the river. Thus ended the ordeal of the river, but not all that we would experience.

Over the next few weeks we kept going, always west and slightly north. Then one day Mrs. Mac stopped as though hit by some bolt of lightning and turned direct north up a small canyon. We traveled from one small canyon to a larger one and then a small one and then larger until we came to a halt against a huge cliff of rocky mountain. Below this rock we could just see amongst the silent snow that drizzled from the clouds, a roof and smoke. The elation of actually seeing that there might be other people near gave us all a spark of hope and an enthusiasm we hadn't realized no longer existed for us. We pushed our horses into a trot, and as the sound of harness echoed through the air, we saw small figures burst from the door of the cabin and begin to wave and shout.

We arrived at the cabin in about fifteen minutes and realized upon arrival that the cabin was dilapidated and worn from years of neglect, but we were greeted with grace and kindness and joy by the two occupants. The man was in his twenties, his long beard attesting to a lack of barbering. His hair was kept in a long braid that descended down his back to the bottom of his buttock. He stepped forward and bowed formally, awkwardly and shyly, like one who has long since forgotten what society requires. 'Hello, friends, welcome to Hollow Valley. This is our home. My name is John Lancaster and this is my sister Norma Lea. Please come in, we have lots of chickens and we can prepare a little supper for you, welcome, welcome.' The young woman beside him wore a dress like none we had seen in years, since we had money. She looked like she was ready for a ball, although the blue satin was slightly dirty and the fine lace suggested either she was deranged or had put this on to impress us. She spoke, 'My brother and I have been here for eight years now. We are the last of our party. We came here looking for a way to Oregon and our party became lost. We ended here when winter set in and decided to stay. It's been that long since we saw an outside face, but come in, it's getting colder and wetter, please join us. Would you all be willing to help with the cooking?'

Over the meal we learned that Norma Lea and John had been the youngest children on their wagon train. Their party had gotten lost in a snowstorm and followed the valleys, thinking they were getting somewhere until they hit the mountains. As the snows grew, the men built one very large cabin for everybody to lodge in and made outbuildings for the cattle and horses. Hard going during the snow, but better than doing nothing. Luckily they had lots of food and were sure that everything would turn out all right. During the winter, it had been decided that, come spring, the men would go back the way they had come and see if they could find a trail that would lead them out of these mountains. The women and the two kids would stay behind. John had wanted to go with the men and had argued bitterly that sixteen made him a man, too, but he was outvoted, and besides they had to leave someone who could protect the women and shoot and take care of the animals. In the end John saw the truth of this. The first two years they had done fine. The cattle roamed the valley and everyone worked together, certain the men would return any moment.

The third winter was harder than the others and some of the cattle froze and had to be eaten. The women began to be depressed and became hopeless that their men would ever return and they wished that they had kept enough horses to hitch up the wagons and go, but that wasn't possible. They made it through the winter and spring, their crops growing, but in the fall after a dry summer, lightning struck at the east end of the valley and the fire that ensued nearly consumed everything that they had built. Everyone took shovels and blankets and water buckets and worked to protect the house and barns. Luckily they had the lake, which was spring fed, at the back of the house, and with everyone working they saved a lot. The cattle and horses had burned in that fire, but they still had lots of chickens. The chickens and the potatoes that survived the fire made up the total of their diet. During the next winter, one of the ladies walked off into the snow during the night and was never found again, although in the spring they found scraps of clothing with blood on them miles from the cabin, probably wolves."

Chapter Nine

"After the fire, hope seemed to disappear, and one by one the women just laid down and died, as though hope drove desire for life.

Norma Lea had been eight when they arrived in Hollow Valley and she was now sixteen. She explained that as the years went by she had altered the different dresses that had been left behind and she was down to only two dresses, one for fancy mourning, a black taffeta, and the one she now wore which was blue satin and lace. She told us she mostly wore buckskin, but put on the party dress because she didn't think we would accept her as white if she greeted us with her tanned skin and jet-black hair. We all laughed and mentioned that once we saw her blue eyes we would have known, but we also had to admit in this part of the world, many shoot first and look second.

On the morning of the second day, Mrs. Mac began to gather her belongings and we all realized that she intended for us to leave. She took Stormy and placed her in the sling that she had created to carry the baby. We all scrambled to get ready, and the dejected looks from John and Norma Lea caught us off guard. We then invited them to join us, and within minutes they stood in front of us with a bag each and their buckskins.

We grabbed some of their harness, what might still be serviceable, and hitched up the old wagon that was half buried in the weeds after years of neglect. Luckily, John had held hope that the men would return for them and each year had cared for and oiled that harness, so that it was mostly good.

As we left the valley, once again heading back the way we had come and almost back to the place we had started, Mrs. Mac turned north and west up a shallow river that no one could imagine would lead anywhere. After two hours of proceeding up the river, we came to a fork in the river and we took the left fork, which was shallower but rockier than we could imagine our wagons would survive. We moved steadily uphill until we seemed to be moving into the clouds of the mountains themselves. The day was cast in dark clouds that forebode either rain or snow and the temperature began to drop. We came to the top of the hill and looked up at the daunting mountains that seemed impassable and death inducing. Mrs. Mac turned directly south along the ridge. We traveled for a couple of hours as the ridge narrowed and rocks fell away along the edge into a deep canyon we could only hear, not see. Our trust in Mrs. Mac began to feel like a wrongness, but there was no room to turn around and the snow began to fall. At first it was slow and pretty, then the sleet began and the wind. Within minutes we were freezing. We broke out blankets and everything warm we had and held on to each other for warmth. We reached what appeared to be the end of the ridge and Mrs. Mac rode off the edge and disappeared. With growing trepidation we came to the edge, and there ten feet below was a broad plateau, big enough for all our wagons, and Mrs. Mac, who was gathering wood for a fire. Even though we still had a lot of daylight, this seemed to be where we would land for the night.

As each wagon dropped that rapid ten-foot embankment, the brakes held and the horses worked hard and we soon had a circle of wagons that seemed to float on the snow and cut out all sense of time and sound.

For the next three days, the blizzard howled and plastered us to our wagons. The fire died in the snow pile and we had to eat cold food and we tried to sleep a lot.

The fourth day dawned sunny and bright, only to show us that the drop from the plateau was an insane step into steep death. We didn't know what we were going to do and this time the inability to speak with Mrs. Mac seemed to be the one thing that would doom us to a long frozen death. Mrs. Mac had somehow managed to milk the cow and feed Stormy and she began to chant and scratch at the snow and every time, she found some wood that might build a fire. Our hardtack was almost gone and the jerky was frozen, our flour was low, and the few potatoes that we had gotten from John and Norma Lea would not keep us long.

Mrs. Mac gave the baby to Ulah May and left us and went back up the ridge. A short time later, she returned with two rabbits. We had seen her do this many times, but no one ever saw a sling or an arrow or marks on the rabbits she always seemed to find. We skinned them and she started a fire, found the big pot in the wagon and put snow, rabbits, potatoes and jerky in the pot. In about an hour, the pot was steaming, and the flavors assaulting our noses made us ready to eat, but each time we thought it was just about right, Mrs. Mac would toss in more snow and the aroma would diminish in direct proportion to the end of steamy water. It felt like she was deliberately torturing us, and yet we could not communicate enough to stop her. After about three hours, she took the ladle and with a question on her face, like 'Okay, you dummies, it's time,' we all raced for our bowls and were gifted with the best tasting thing we had had in months.

Of course, we had just had our fill of fried chicken less than a week before. But when you're frozen and in the snow, the memory of fried chicken fails to maintain its flavor and the now becomes far more real.

After everyone had gotten their fill, Mrs. Mac added more snow and the pot appeared almost to be full again. It dawned on us all that this was to be our food for several days and we needed to conserve it. Sometimes in the joy of the moment, we forget that the future must be considered as well as the present.

The second day found us still on the plateau and we had no clue what was next, but as usual Mrs. Mac began to pack up and we all hustled up and got the horses and cows and the people together to head out.

We started up the ten-foot embankment, the footing slippery for the horses, and proceeded along the ridge-top a couple of miles and there on the downside and the west side was a trail that you could never see, much less actually turn onto from the other direction. The trail was slippery with frozen snow, but as the wagons broke through and the hooves of the horses drove down into it they managed to grip but not slide.

At the end of the day, we were in the bottom. As we headed south, we all wondered if there was even the vague possibility of there being a way through. We camped that night listening to the wolves shrieking at the full moon that cast strange shadows and luminous light on a landscape that was so foreign to us that we felt like we had left planet earth and landed somewhere where black replaced green and only snow and cold embraced man with a whisper of the invitation of death."

Chapter Ten

"The next day we traveled further south and the land got no more hospitable than it had been before. On the third day we came to a wide river that was frozen over and Mrs. Mac turned west and south upon it. As the wagons traveled, we could hear the ice crack and we all began to mumble the prayer that we had come to use in time of need, 'Please, God, let there be a place for us, a place where we belong.'

We traveled all day and through the night, into the mad moonlight and howling wolves. We so wanted to stop, but Mrs. Mac never got off the horse, not even to feed the baby nor milk the moaning cow.

As dawn broke through on the second day of travel, a space widened on the left bank of the river and the sharp cliffs parted, even if just momentarily, and Mrs. Mac climbed the bank and dismounted. We followed and by the time we had unharnessed the exhausted horses, a fire was going and the pot of frozen soup was on the fire and Mrs. Mac had milked the cow and was feeding a very hungry Stormy.

We spent the day there, sleeping and the horses dug the snow away from the dry grass that was to be their only sustenance for the day. These amazing creatures, the horse is the gift and the helpmate to man, and we take for granted that he will always give to us and survive on what we don't provide.

At nightfall, Mrs. Mac mounted again. We all wanted to object, we were still exhausted from the last night of travel and to start again seemed like a cruelty to us and the horses. The cold that night was so depressing that we all dreaded going again, but we went. We traveled up the river all that night, following the woman with the sleeping baby and knowing that she had to have a reason, even if we didn't get what it was. Another frosty dawn and she kept moving, the warmth of the sun a wonderful gift to our frozen bodies and feet.

We traveled until mid afternoon, when we noticed that the ice was getting wet from the melt caused by the sun and the cracks in the ice which had become almost comforting in their regularity, were starting to pop rather loudly. We rounded a bend in the river and there on the right was a wide opening between the mountains and Mrs. Mac rode up the bank to it. The wagons began to slide as we tried to negotiate that embankment and the horses strained at the collars, trying to keep their feet and also to bring the wagons around. The scream of the ice as the last wagon worked to land shattered all of us with the sound of the ice breaking beneath the wagon. Ulah May and Lulah May were riding in that wagon and John Lancaster was driving. The fear that we all felt was written on their faces, but John grabbed the whip and struck with such intensity that the horses leapt forward with an energy even they did not know they had, and the back wheels hit solid earth at the edge of the river and the horses plunged ahead with a spark of life that was the second wind for a racehorse.

As we all pulled up on the grass and snow we got down and hugged one another and blessed John for what he had done, and Ulah and Lulah kissed him so much he began to blush. Norma Lea was blessing and kissing the horses while all this was going on and the stoic Mrs. Mac, who seldom had any expression for us, looked on with the smile and pride of a mother hen for her baby chicks."

Chapter Eleven

"We rested there for two days. Only as the ice began to melt and break did we finally understand the gift that Mrs. Mac had given us. If we hadn't traveled during the snow and the cold, we would have sunk in the river and drowned. We all thanked and blessed Mrs. Mac, though she appeared not to understand what we were saying, we knew that the energy was palpable.

On the third morning, we once again set out for the destination unknown and we still asked for the place we belonged to show up soon.

After another week of travel, we ran out of food. We couldn't eat the cow, 'cause we needed milk for Stormy, the bull had drowned with Mathilda and the others; the only choice left was the calf. We slaughtered him and ate him and made jerky for the rest of the trip. It was obvious to all that the little food we had left would not last more than five days for all of us, so the boys Jed, John and

Joshua took off to see if they could scare up a deer or a boar or some rabbits.

We traveled for three more weeks and the land had more tall trees and wide meadows. We struggled and rested more in order to find food. The rest was good for the horses, because they began to fatten as the grass turned green with spring. We all began to look like scarecrows, even though the boys brought back meat, it would have been nice to have some flour and salt and sugar, all of which were gone.

One morning we awoke to find ourselves with company. Two Indians, one was tall and the feather headdress he wore was fascinating, the other was shorter and he wore a helmet and breastplate that looked like the conquistadors. They began to speak to us, their English had no accent and their speech was very clear.

'Welcome friends, we have been waiting for you. Your coming was told to us many moons before the snow came, we welcome you. This is the place you have been looking for. We have food for you and warm waters to rest your bodies in. Please follow us.'

Only Norma Lea looked at us and said, 'Did you hear them talking?' Of course, we had all heard them talk and then Norma Lea said, 'Didn't you notice that their mouths didn't move?' We had all been so fascinated by them and their outfits that no one had noticed."

Chapter Twelve

"As we moved along behind the two men, Mrs. Mac rode along with them. They did not seem to be talking so maybe they spoke a different language. About midday, we arrived at a small settlement of teepees. There were no children in this encampment, only middle-aged and old people. The place had an air of longevity and sadness that we did not understand, but we were glad for the happiness that they all had at our arrival. As we stepped from the wagons and began to unharness our horses, they gathered around Stormy and became excited by the small child who began to laugh as though she were being tickled. This was a sound that none of us had heard from her before, as she definitely was her namesake.

The women of the tribe embraced Mrs. Mac like one of their own and then a man, the youngest in the group walked over to her and embraced her with a warmth that is usually saved for family, and her smile indicated that she felt the same way about him. He walked over to us and in a slight accent began to speak. 'Welcome friends, I am Running Elk, this is my mother. You call her Mrs. Mac. She has told me of my father's passing and much of your journey. We have food prepared, after you eat we will take you to the bathing pools so that the waters may refresh and nurture your bodies. The men will take your horses to the best grass; do not worry, they will not leave. This is their home as well as yours.'

Until he had said this was our home, we had not even considered that, indeed this place felt different than anything we had ever felt and there was truly a very peaceful familiarity to it, as though we had always been here.

The food that they had for us was venison and something that tasted like chicken, but had a softer quality and no bones. The vegetables and the nuts were unfamiliar, but after weeks of none, they tasted like we had died and gone to heaven. They had a strange sort of bread-like substance that was flat and round and best of all, there was salt available and a sweet substance that we later learned was honey based and special to these people."

Chapter Thirteen

"After dinner, Running Elk came and said, 'Would you now please come to the bathing pools, they are natural springs of hot water that will nurture and heal your bodies and you will sleep very peacefully after you have been in them.' We all rose together and followed Running Elk up a small incline and then down to a bend in the river that flowed through the valley and was a major part of the life here. Ulah May asked, 'So, what do you call this place?' 'We call this simply 'the place,'' replied Running Elk. We all just sort of nodded and realized that we were far more bone-weary than we had realized. As we came to the steaming waters that ran from a pool that was surrounded by boulders, we were told that if we desired hotter water we had only to climb up a few boulders and we would find a pool that was hotter higher up. None of us had ever seen this kind of place and we didn't understand really what hot water was, the best any of us had experienced was the tub that was drug in the house and we took turns boiling water in buckets and taking it in and adding it to the water that was already cold from the well, this looked like it had to be hotter than any bucket off the stove and it was a large pool that could have fit all our wagons and the horses and still have had room for us.

All of the village came to the pool, and as they arrived they all took their clothes off as though it was perfectly normal to get naked in front of strangers. For most of us taking off clothes was only done when you were goin' to change to a new outfit. Even when takin' a bath most kept their undergarments on and only washed them off first and then wrapped with a towel. Here were all these Indian folk strippin' down and walkin' into the water. It seemed so natural that most of the youngsters just went for it. The rest of us hesitated and then began to figure out how to avoid this without being rude.

The two men that had met us on the road appeared and stood in front of us and began to take off their clothes. As they did they began to speak very softly and to chant. As this began, we sort of lost all inhibitions and began to shuck our clothes like we had done this forever. Once agin, Norma Lea whispered, 'They still aren't moving their lips, but I can hear them talking,' and this time several of the rest of us noticed the same thing. When we looked back on it later, we realized we should have questioned it and we should have had at least a little propriety left that would make us not just strip down in front of total strangers, especially since most of us had never even seen each other buck naked, but we didn't. We sort of felt like children whose curiosity overcame their senses, and we stared unashamedly at the naked people who were getting into the pool. It's odd when you look back and realize that none of what should have been going through our minds as God-fearing Christians, actually even existed. The most unique thing that we all later found astounding, was that the bodies of all the people here, no matter the age, were not wrinkled or sagging. Maybe it was just because they were Indians, but all the white folks we had ever known had sags and wrinkles by the time they hit fifty. None of these people looked to have aged at all, and in the fading light of sunset, telling which was which, became an extreme difficulty.

As the dark descended and the new moon began to rise, gifting only a shadowy awareness of the people soaking in this miraculous water, we began to sit back against the hot rocks and relax. Swimming holes during the hot, muggy summers of Georgia had been a joy in the refreshment of coolness, but these pools with their hot waters and the calmness we all felt, began to ease away the stiffness and soreness that we had become so accustomed to that we hadn't realize they existed, until these soft and caressing waters allowed them to seep away."

Chapter Fourteen

"Ryan Boyle, who was married to Lulah May, had sort of become the leader of our group, and he felt that it was his job to find out what he could from the leaders of this group, like were we safe here, who did we need to worry about and what did they expect of us. He had managed to keep track of the two who had first met us, but realized that he had no idea what their names were. As he moved across the pond to sit in the empty spot next to them, we all heard them say, 'I am Tall Feathers and my friend is called Ancient One.' (We had no question about who was who.) 'You must know that we have been expecting you. Jonathan MacDonald and Mrs. Mac came to find you. We heard your pleas for a place many moons ago, and they came for you. Mac was the last person to seek us, that was many seasons in the past, and Running Elk is his son. Running Elk is the last child that was born to us. 'The place' is the safest spot on earth. It cannot be found by accident, you only come to it from your need and from your request, what you would call your prayers. We expect nothing of you, we only request that you carry on the traditions of this place and make it your own.'

Ryan spoke loudly so all could hear, 'What are the traditions here and what do we have to give you for this land?'

Again Tall Feathers spoke softly, 'There is no payment for this land, as we do not own it, it owns us. We are only the stewards of this land, it nurtures and cares for us, not the other way around. It gifted itself to us and now it invites you to be nurtured by it.'

'Let us explain,' said Ancient One, 'longer ago that I can recall, my people came to be attacked by the ones who wore the armor I now possess. These people were cruel and vicious in their pursuit of the gold metal that my people found and used for decorations. My people were pursued by these people, and as we ran away, we asked for a place of safety that they could not find. My ancestors, after one last fight, the one that gave my grandfather the armor, fled and found 'the place.' The families lived here for long years, but slowly as many grew very old—but none looked old—they discovered that no children came. By your time, my people lived hundreds of years and I am the last of my tribe. Tall Feathers is my son, he is by your time hundreds of years old, it is only when someone new arrives that we can increase our numbers. Only those that ask to find 'the place' can come to it and they, as the new, can have children. It has been over 100 years since the last people came to 'the place' and that was Mac. We have had no new children in 100 years, and the people are sad and have asked for the new to come to replace them. With your arrival, many will now go to the Great Spirit, as they have completed their promise to the land. It will be their choice to leave. Several have already decided to leave, but many are curious to see the new children that you will create.'

'If you choose to honor the land, then you will agree to stay and you will live hundreds of years and have children with only those that are new. It will be difficult and joyful at the same time. You will always have the right to leave and many will. Most will be gone for periods of not more than forty years and then will return to remain for the rest of their lives. It is always choice, but few places on earth will nurture and care for you the way 'the place' does.'

We all sat stunned, not wanting to believe, wishing to believe that the old man was lying and at the same time, the lightness of the telling disintegrated all the skepticism that we could muster, and the simplicity and truth of what was being said seemed greater than real.

There was no further talk that night and we all went to bed, dragging ourselves from the pool, relaxed almost to the inability to move, and crawled into our beds, bunks, bedrolls, or even in the tents with the Indians on the soft fur of animals as yet unknown to us. None of us thought that night, and by morning we were out of doubt and into total curiosity and need of other possibilities. It is remarkable that when one hears that which is true, it creates a sense of lightness and rightness, and when one hears a lie, it always feels heavy. The night had made the truth brighter and the trust in these people was palpable. We had made our commitment to the land without even a discussion, and somehow we all knew it. There was never a discussion from that day forward that required a vote, we all just knew what each of us thought about everything."

Chapter Fifteen

Uncle Jed had told his story over three days. Each day had ended with my falling asleep as he rubbed my feet. The last day, however, had scratched my scab of skepticism to a raw edge. I knew he believed this crap, but I sure wasn't going there. How the hell could anybody with an ounce of sense believe this crap was true? The door creaked again and there was beautiful Ruth with breakfast. It smelled good and she looked good and I still wanted to believe that the world was as normal as it was before the accident. "Good morning, Ruth, what's for breakfast?"

"Good morning, Jacob. I think you're beautiful, too. Breakfast today is eggs and venison steak. Will that suit you? Today the rest of our community would like to introduce themselves to you. Would that be all right for you?"

"I didn't realize there were other people here. How come I can't feel them the way I feel you, Uncle Jed and the boys?"

“Jacob, they did not wish to confuse your healing and they wanted you to become comfortable, so kept their presence from you merely to make sure you were well on the way before you had to add them to the pieces of what it means to be in ‘the place’.”

“Can they come in and introduce themselves now?”

As the door creaked open, a stunning woman in her mid-thirties or early forties entered the door. ”Hi, I’m Stormy Lancaster and this is my husband John.”

“Hello, Jacob, my name is Running Elk,” he says as he reaches to shake my hand. As he shakes my hand, I feel a strange slip occur as though the bed has moved and then gone back to where it belongs. I feel Running Elk the way I felt the boys and then Uncle Jed and Ruth, and my world expands in some way I can’t describe.

“And this must be Norma Lea,” I say in my best sarcastic voice.

She laughs and I know she is laughing at me, and for some reason I like it and begin to laugh with her. With the laughter, the need to be a skeptic vanishes and I realize that there is some vague recognition of all these people that I can only put down to a sense of belonging, and yet the lack of the sense that this is real or normal haunts the back of my mind, and the dictator of the past screams this can’t be so and I shouldn’t believe. “Jacob,” says Norma Lea, “Everything that you have heard from Jed is real. I know how hard it is to believe that people can live for hundreds of years and not age greatly, doesn't function in what you call 'the real world,' but you might want to consider that even the Bible talks about people living to be hundreds of years old. We are the living expression of that possibility."

I don't know what to say, and my brain is spinning at the idea that this is real. I look for inconsistencies and that apparent lack of aging alone leaves this sketchy at best. I want to believe that this is some enormous scam, but I don't have lots of money and the awareness of what I have and have had with Ruth makes it seem greater than real. How do I reconcile what I've known as reality and the different reality that is being presented now?

Norma Lea steps over to the bed and leans down and kisses my forehead. Again that strange feeling of the bed moving and the world sliding, and I know I can feel her, and with it comes an awareness of all the people in this village and also the feel of the trees and the plants and the animals, and as I close my eyes, I can sense the world outside for miles around, and the river and the hot springs and the cabins and the thousand other things that have a sense of being and awareness of self that I thought only belonged to mankind.

Running Elk steps towards me and sits on the bed, friendly sorts aren't they? I didn't even invite anyone to sit down, and they all sit on the chairs around the room.

"Jacob, we don't desire you to accept what is our reality—skepticism and confusion come from not enough information. Norma Lea has just opened you to a level of awareness that is but the beginning of what you will know and what is available to you. We are here to give you the information you require, but we cannot give it to you unless you ask us. Information given unbidden rots and putrefies in the mind if it is not cleansed with the awareness of what you either already know or what you can recognize as truth."

The slight accent that matches the story that Uncle Jed has been feeding me is so very real it confuses and intrigues me. "Okay, so how many of you are there here and how many of you were born before 1860?"

Chapter Sixteen

"There are twenty-eight of us that were born prior to 1860 and another fifty that are part of our group or have been born since. Some of the fifty have found 'the place' during their time of request. Not all of our group are currently with us, there are some that go into the outside world so that they can find those that look for us, though often they do not know for what they search.

You tell me how many there are in the camp currently. You can use your senses to count or you can just allow the knowing to fill your mind with the answer."

I drift into that place I had with the ducklings and the creek, and suddenly as if by magic I know that there are sixty-seven people present.

"Yes, Jacob, that is correct, there are sixty-seven of us currently present in our compound," says John.

This is the first time I have heard John speak, the accent he bears is so much like Ruth's, I feel like there is something I should know, but I can't put my finger on it. "Okay, I have a question. How come, if you all are supposed to be the same age as Uncle Jed, he looks so much older than the rest of you?"

John speaks. "Well, as we have discovered, there are some that search for a different possibility in life, you were one of those. Always they ask for the place they belong. Jed decided about 1916 that he wanted to go see some of the world and he left here to find some adventure. After living in the same place for fifty years, it does necessitate leaving occasionally. He had already left for small periods earlier but had always returned with a sense the world was a pretty crazy place and that with time it might get better. One of the most difficult parts of living with the awareness we have here is that after a while you can feel what is happening around the world, and the places where war and famine are occurring hurt as much as if we were there ourselves. At any rate, Jed left in 1918, knowing that what you call World War I would soon be over and wishing to take the healing he could do to the world, and he set out to find those that would need him when modern medicine failed. He got a job in a hospital for those that had suffered mental collapse during the war, and he was an orderly for them. As the people under his care began to have miracle healings and come out of their disconnected states, rumors began to spread that he was a faith healer.

One day a woman came to the hospital, Jed appeared to be about twenty-five at the time and this lady was thirty. Jed took one look at her and knew this was the woman that would have his children and become as important to him as breathing. Her brother was in the hospital, in a different ward and was pretty much so disconnected that they weren't sure he would ever be okay again, and they were trying to get her to move him to an insane asylum so that they wouldn't have to deal with him at all. Lenora was her name and she had come from a family that had been tent revivalists for many years. The orderlies liked Lenora as she was kind and caring in a time when most were angry. They told her about the odd man who kept getting patients better when the doctors could not, and she sought him out.

Jed had already had some trouble with a couple of the doctors, but the nurses had received so much help and seen so many recover that they were doing everything to protect him.

Lenora came and looked into his face and realized that this was the true thing, that God had indeed sent an angel to help her. They went for a walk in the gardens and after three hours of conversation she convinced Jed to help. The doctors in Leonard's ward had Jed ejected when he showed up to visit with Lenora, apparently his reputation had gone farther than he realized.

Lenora invited Jed to come to their house and live with them and agreed to pay him for what he might do for her brother. He agreed, in truth, the money and all the rest were as nothing, he would have paid to stay with her.

Lenora had Leonard moved to the house and Jed moved in. It took two days for Leonard to get calm and another four months for him to become functional. During those months, the angel became a devil in some ways and Lenora was captured, body and soul. Six months later they were married and Leonard sang and danced and laughed with and for them.

Eight months later the first of their children, Rebecca, was born, it was April 1, 1920.

Over the next six years, there were three more children that came and with each, the longing increased in Jed to return to 'the place.' Over the years Jed had spoken about the place but had never mentioned his real age, and he so loved her that he continually bought her need to be with her family and stay in the family home that her great-grandfather had built. He realized he could never get her to believe that what he could do was based on anything but God's love and gifts.

In 1926, Leonard married a lovely young woman named Barbara and within a year their daughter Ruth was born.

In the stock market crash, the family fortune disappeared and the only thing left was the house. The two couples and the kids moved in together and began to take in boarders to create some income. The family home sat on twenty acres of land and the adults began to plant crops. It all seemed to be sitting pretty good until the rabbits discovered the tender shoots of succulent squash and lettuce and the tops of carrots, which quit growing when you clip their greens. Meat was hard to come by, and there wasn't enough money to pay the grocer, so Jed talked the butcher into trading flour for rabbits. Luckily he had learned Mrs. Mac's trick of talking the rabbits into sacrificing themselves to help the family. And so the comfort level rose for the couples and their children."

Chapter Seventeen

I awoke to the sound of the fire crackling. It must be cold outside if the fire is lit. I wonder when it was started, I can see through the curtains that are drawn and sense the cold that is apparent in the darkness of the sky that this would be a great day for reading and snuggling in bed.

I think of my son and the door creaks open and Roy walks in with a load of logs.

"Hi Roy, how's it going? Is it really cold outside?" Of course, when he opened the door I had felt the chill of the wind.

"Mr. Rayne, you're funny, you already know that answer and sense the change in the weather, so why do you ask such silly things?"

I realize that he's right, in my other world you say inane things as though that's what's necessary to have communication, and I am aware suddenly that I will have to choose a different way to be with people who actually already know what I know, and we don't have to pretend that it's not possible to have total awareness of everything that is available to us.

"You know, Mister Rayne... okay, I will call you Jake if you like, we do know and we don't want to freak you out so whatever is necessary for you to say, we will honor your need... and Rob and I like to mess with people a bit so we will let you know what you need to know about what you know that we already know, if you know what I mean?"

His smile says it all. The sweetness and gentleness with which I have just been put in my place amuses me no end and I laugh from that intense sweet joy that I only thought came with my child. As the laughter dies, I wonder if the boys are the ones who laid the fire in the first place and came in that strange way that does not depend on doors or walls to cooperate.

"Jake, you're wrong when you think that the doors and walls don't cooperate. They are molecules like us that vibrate to create the seen world and because of that, we have to vibrate at the same rate as them for them not to keep us from moving as the space we are in collaboration with their vibration so they will let us move through them, as you call it."

"Thanks, Roy, I always feel like I am years behind you in what you know and how you function with a world I want to believe exists, but it's just so hard to think that everything is the opposite of what it appears to be."

"Jake, what you believe is what stops what you can perceive and know. Your beliefs are what you chose in order to understand the world as everyone saw it and told you it was. Here we function without beliefs, but from total awareness, so we don't have to believe that we can doubt in order to believe in that what isn't actually true must be true."

"Roy, you sound like the philosophy professor I had in college, only he always tried to tell me I had to believe in what I couldn't see. It's very odd to talk with a twelve year old, who knows more than the harbingers of wisdom."

"Who says I'm twelve?"

Chapter Eighteen

And with that he disappears. I guess he's right, I only assumed he had to be twelve because that's the way his body appears, but if Stormy appears to be twenty-five to thirty and she was born in the 1860s, then the boys would be much older than they appear and so must everyone else.

The door creaks and "she" enters with another tray of bacon and eggs, and I sense that there is some kind of great smelling and feeling toast.

"Good Morning, Jacob. How are you feeling today?"

Suddenly I realize that she knows how I feel and that these questions never have to be asked here. I wonder about this beautiful woman that I have known and been part of for so long, what should I say, and what do I have to say and where does one begin.

"Jacob, I already know what you think and I have all the awareness of you that I will ever need as long as we are together. Perhaps it would be that you should ask me some questions to give you the clarity you desire and the peace that comes with the certainty of what you only suspect."

Suddenly I recall the story about Jed and his love, Lenora, and how Leonard and Barbara had had a daughter named Ruth in 1928. No, it can't be, if that were true, though she looks to be my age, she has to be almost three times my age.

"Yes, Jacob, Barbara and Leonard were my parents, and though I've been on earth longer than you that doesn't necessarily mean we are older."

"Okay Ruth, now you are going to have to tell the rest of the story that John and Running Elk started the other day."

Chapter Nineteen

She sets the tray down on the bed, and as I begin to eat I experience a sense that time and space are changing, and that after this conversation and meal, everything that I have believed will have disappeared.

"Jacob, when I was eight years old, my parents were killed in an auto accident, and I was already living with Uncle Jed and Aunt Lenora, and Rebecca and I felt more like sisters than cousins, all of us kids did everything together.

Aunt Lenora hated the depression and had so much difficulty using the family home as a boarding house that Uncle Jed decided he had to do something about it. One of the abilities he had discovered as a young man was the ability to find metal objects buried in the ground. The family home is on the east coast and was built on the site of a famous Civil War battleground. Uncle Jed began to find old metal objects for Aunt Lenora, and she knew some families that were collectors from the days when they had money, and she would sell them. One of Uncle Jed's journeys led him into the woods that bordered the main road and he found a strong box buried there. It contained $4,000 in gold coins. A fortune during that time, and though they could never figure out whether it belonged to someone specific or to some mobster that got killed, it put the family back into a place of having money. With that money, Aunt Lenora went out into the neighborhood and the neighboring towns and bought antiques that people had left in attics and barns. She knew about these from the times she had spent traveling after the First World War.

Since her family had been part of the wealthy set, she also knew about jewelry and she began to find people who wanted to sell, and she would travel to New York to connect with old friends who still had money and sell the things she found. My dad and mom also got in on the system and soon developed a clientele of their own. Dad's old war buddies had money and jobs, and he and mom were able to buy a car that made it easier to find and move the antiques and jewelry they found. That's how they got killed. They were driving back from a buying trip in Chicago when the police started to chase some bootleggers. One of the police shot dad by accident and the car went off the road and mom was killed.

After that, life changed for me, and Aunt Lenora lost momentum and began to avoid going out of the house. Uncle Jed had become rather good at finding things and buying them reasonably, and where Aunt Lenora had been known as a sharp buyer and a seller who could always get top dollar, Uncle Jed became known as a man who was fair to a fault on both sides. It was odd to Aunt Lenora that he would pay more and sell for less and they continually got richer.

In 1941, the Japanese attacked Pearl Harbor. Uncle Jed's sons signed up as soon as they could. The oldest was nineteen the day of the attack and two days later he signed up. That was Harry. His younger brother had to wait until his eighteenth birthday, which was May 1942. They went off to war much against the wishes of Uncle Jed, who could feel the travesty that war is much more than others do.

In 1943 on some island in the South Pacific, Harry was killed. His body was delivered to our home and he was buried in the family plot. Aunt Lenora was devastated and began to pray every day that God would save Henry from the disaster that he faced.

Rebecca's boyfriend Jimmy decided it was time for him to join up and she insisted that they get married immediately. The wedding was beautiful in the springtime garden of the family home and five days later he left for the war. Nine months to the day their first child, Damon, was born. Aunt Lenora finally came out of her depression, as the child was everything that promised hope and future.

Henry was killed on D-day and Aunt Lenora took to her bed for the next forty years, she was never fully functional but always appeared to be wasting away as she slipped through the house like a ghost.

Rebecca's husband came home for the funeral on leave and he and Rebecca determined that their child would be better off if they found their own place after he returned. Christine, the youngest of the clan, had decided that the family home was cursed and that she was going to New York to live and that no one would ever get her to come back to this cursed place to live ever again. Uncle Jed pleaded, while Aunt Lenora smiled benignly and serenely, unaware of what was occurring. Christine refused to listen and she stormed from the housing yelling that Uncle Jed was a fool and that her mother was only bad luck and death embodied. She never returned to that house again."

Chapter Twenty

As Ruth told the story, I watched and felt the sensation of suffering that made my life, loves and divorce pretty meaningless. I also understood the look of age and wisdom that was part of Uncle Jed. I could only imagine what it would be like to lose children at such an early age and know that there is nothing you can do.

"So, what happened to Rebecca? Uncle Jed said that she gave up before the twins were born. How did that happen?"

"Jacob, that visit home from Rebecca's husband produced the twins."

My head begins to spin again, because if that is so then the twins are actually a product of the war and not twelve years old at all.

"You are correct, Jacob. The twins are the product of Rebecca's love, and she cared for him so much that when he was killed in a plane crash in

Greenland on his way to Europe, she determined that death was a welcome shadow in the home of her family.

During her pregnancy, Uncle Jed decided that it was important to take me and Rebecca to visit his relatives out west. We had never heard of these relatives and were both intrigued and perplexed that this had never been part of our family history. We had all sort of assumed that Uncle Jed was just an orphan or something since he had never talked about his family.

He packed us in the car and headed for the west coast; Aunt Lenora was none too happy to see us leave, but there was a wonderful black lady who had come to live with us after Henry died, she was the mother of one of his buddies who had been killed at the same time. She had no more family, so she came to take care of ours. Her name was Katie and she somehow understood Aunt Lenora better than anyone, including Uncle Jed.

We came to the road that led to 'the place' late one afternoon and we stopped the car just after we passed a stand of trees and the road sort of ended. Standing there in the shadows of the late afternoon were about thirty people. We didn't understand how they knew to be there, and like you, we had a lot of learning to do about the difference between them and the rest of the world.

The peace of this place was a balm to my soul and for the first time since my parents died, I had a sense that life could actually be good and joyful.

Rebecca, with each passing day became more distraught, the folks all tried to show her that losing her husband was not the end of her life but the beginning for her boys. How they all knew that she was having twins was never doubted but never explained either. Uncle Jed spent many long days showing her the place and walking in the woods and taking her to the pools, all in an attempt to tease her back to the beauty of life. I went with them most of the time and looked and saw and felt the magnificence of what this place is. I began to heal.

Rebecca and I lived in this very cabin back then and we shared that bed. Each night we would talk, and I realized in about the eighth month that her will for life was leaving. She spoke of wanting to be with Harry and Henry and "her Jimmy." I told Uncle Jed and he took me in his arms and told me that we would have to honor her choice. He had tried so hard to convince her and heal her, and like with Aunt Lenora, ultimately he could not change what they did not want to change.

After the twins were born, and the labor was only two hours, she handed the babies to me and asked if I would take them and raise them as though they were mine. Through my tears and pleading, I sat with her as she passed from this realm.

The boys, Rob and Roy, have been my charge since that day, April 29, 1947, but they have been the delight of the entire group to raise, and with all of the different energies and awareness that were shared, they have developed some of the special abilities that you have experienced.

Well, I guess that's probably a lot to take in right now, so I'll leave and see you in the morning." She moves from the room with that intense grace and fluidity that leaves me breathless and missing her and once again, I feel as though I am being kissed and caressed as the door slides silently shut.

Chapter Twenty-One

Uncle Jed enters my room, funny that now this seems like "my room" just because I have occupied it for so long.

"Well, Jacob, you've learned a lot about us in the last few weeks, what else do you need to know in order to give up the last parts of your skepticism?"

As Uncle Jed touches my feet and that strange feeling of the molecules clanging together begins, I realize that I still don't understand why Jed is the only old person here.

"Jacob, one of the things that we have learned over time about 'the place' is that as long as you stay here, you don't age much and that if you leave, as long as you are not gone for more that forty years, you still don't age. When I found Lenora, I promised to spend the rest of her life with her. After the boys died, she lost touch with reality and no matter how much I tried to get her to come here, she wanted to stay in her home. After Christine moved to New York and Lenora began to drift away and Rebecca had her babies here, I knew that I had to return to Lenora. I lived with her for the next forty years, in a house that I maintained, and as she got older, she forgot that I was her husband and decided I was the butler and handyman. Christine never came to see her mother; occasionally, I would get a letter from her and find out about her life. She never married and lived as an actress and star on Broadway. I loved her, but she had changed her name so no one would know where she had come from, and she made up stories, so that she could invent herself. I loved her letters and always asked if she would let me come and see her, but she always said no. Ultimately, I lost all of my children, but I still have the boys, my grandsons."

Uncle Jed takes his hands off my feet and the strange sensation of the molecules clanging together gathers and grows and my body begins to feel more like space and less weighty than ever before.

"Would you like to take a short walk today, Jacob?"

The instant and intense joy that my body exudes even without my thoughts or desires, gives me the odd sense that there is some life force within my body that has chosen without my needs being asked, required or considered. I have never felt this energy and aliveness before. "Yes, absolutely!"

Uncle Jed laughs that wonderful rolling laughter that cleanses your soul and sends shock waves up your body, and he takes my hand.

"Now, Jacob, you need to take it slow, you have done a lot of healing, but there are still some things that have to shift back to where they were, to get the total blood flow and energy flow that actually heals a body."

He takes my legs and pulls them gently towards the edge of the bed and begins to slide them off the edge while pulling on the left arm, and my body begins to move into the sitting position it has not experienced for at least six weeks. As I finally achieve the upright position and put the weight on my buttocks, an ice pick slices up my spine piercing my brain with the jagged edges of desire for unconsciousness that reminds me and my body of the night on the road. I start to slip towards the sanctuary of darkness that is my refuge from pain, but Uncle Jed jolts me back to presence with the intense rolling movement of the molecules in my back and spine and brain that enrolls the molecules to clang louder than before and to become what can only be described as the space of space within space of the body.

"Now it's time to stand, but don't move too fast and allow me to handle that weight and movement of your body."

As I try to lift myself, there is no certainty in my world that the muscles will actually work. I realize that I decided I would never walk again the first morning I awoke and had no feeling in my legs. Odd that would come to me at this moment, and then I realize that was the way everything was working in my life, prior to 'the place,' and every time I decided that something was going to be a certain way, that's exactly what would show up. Ever since being here, what I thought was true has been turned upside down and I can suddenly see that nothing I have ever thought was true or real; nothing was anything other than proving that what I believed was real was real. I began to laugh as Uncle Jed held my arms and pulled me off the bed and onto my feet. The feel of the floor was like touching moss that grows in the winter— wet, and it made velvet seem rough and shallow in the multiple flavors of life and softness and moisture that embraces and speaks and thrills at the gift that you receive as it gifts to you with every molecule of its being. The floor, which I had thought was some strange inanimate object seduces, embraces and gifts the molecules of energy that is its life, not was its life, and every step as I move across the floor energizes, heals and inspirits my body and being. Uncle Jed laughs again, that rolling, healing, exuberance of light and life, and my body tingles even more. This sensation is like being a new baby, where each and every moment is so amusing, embracing and nurturing that life begins to desire itself in the body and the soul.

As we go for the door, Jed begins to hum. I don't mean like in humming a tune, but rather like his body is exuding a frequency of vibration that is viscerally apparent though not audibly perceived. The door opens by itself and we step into the bright light of a day that is cold and invigorating with a light spray of snow littering the ground. I start to think, "But I have no shoes" and I suddenly realize that the cold is like a blanket of welcome and the snow beneath my feet is nurturing to the very cells of the earth and to me. I don't "feel the snow" but rather the intense sense of the caring that the snow is, not as a wrongness from warm, but rather the difference of enjoyment and the zing of life strikes again with the exuberance of a bouncing puppy. My body moves with each step stronger and more enthusiastic for the song of life that, like the hum of Uncle Jed, strokes, caresses and nurtures the body and the being, and each moment the orchestra of the trees and the wind and the birds and the silence and the space that includes all the people of "the place," who, like me now, are the cathedral of oneness, the whisper of possibilities and the joy of difference awakened to the elements of molecular harmony and vibrational coherence that heresies and spiritual enlightenment have spoken of but never given nor demonstrated. I have never been so aware and so space and so totally cared for in my life, and I know now that "the place" and I own one another with an unparalleled freedom and peace that I have dreamed and desired and sought but never found. I am home, I am me and I am expanded from the ordinary to the phenomenal without an ounce of negative energy available or real any longer.

The boys appear and as Uncle Jed lets go of my hands, they take over and instantly I am back in my bed. They cover me with blankets and are gone in the next heartbeat. I am alone, but not alone. The peace that I now know is truly me eliminates the idea that alone is any more real than the other crazy rightness I used to define the limits of life. How does one exist in the world when everything that isn't real—but only your ideas and beliefs bought from parents, family, schools and relationships make them appear real—is what defines your choice and your coffin of reality?

I realize now that the world I have left has so little substance it is like reading a comic book, in which the pictures explain the story and the motivation for every action is based on the stupidity and lack of communication and awareness and the pretenses and proofs of caring, not the peace and space that I now know is a truer caring than I ever thought possible. Oh blessed peace and joyful space, thanks for including me in the knowing of what is greater and giving me the gift of recognizing that I never have to make myself less again.

Chapter Twenty-Two

I awaken, perceiving the snow that now covers the ground, I even know that it is two feet deep, and I can perceive the rabbits and rodents sleeping and moving and the hawks and owls that forage in the snow for the unaware who do not go beyond their senses but function from their need and hunger.

The door silently opens and Ruth enters, a warm skin jacket wraps around the luscious body I long to touch and her embarrassment proves once again that she knows what I think.

The tray is larger today and I realize that we are going to eat together. The small table under the window becomes the invitation for my body to exit the bed and sit in a chair for a change. I would like to be tentative about getting up, but I know that it would be a true lie that I can't do it. My legs swing off the bed just like they did when I was fifteen and discovered that running got rid of cobwebs and relieved the stress that hormones rattling my brain and racking my body seemed to be the eternal battle for dominance of mind over matter.

"It's good to have you up and about. The boys put you back to bed at the moment that your body had reached the maximum receiving it could tolerate with moving to pain. There is a place where the intensity of what can be experienced has been misinterpreted as pain for most people and they assume that the intensity cannot actually be included as part of awareness and mankind calls that pain. If you would like, today we can go to the pools where the hot waters will heal and nurture you and your body."

"I can think of something else that sounds nurturing and healing to my body. Perhaps we could consider that instead?"

Her laugh and sparkling eyes tell everything. She's not against it, but it's not happening today. Wow, I just realize that I actually picked that up from her thoughts not her eyes and mannerisms.

We eat and she rises, puts on some boots that I haven't noticed before and offers to put some on me. As she places the boots, which are soft and pliable, on my feet, I wonder how these will take the snow. She smiles and once again her thoughts give me the whole story, and I know that these will never absorb the snow or the cold because of the energy we will provide to them.

We leave that cabin and begin to walk through the snow. My new awareness of the life and beauty of everything around me fills my senses and the silence that the new snow carries assaults my every molecule with the inordinate graciousness that the elements gift and we so miserly ignore. For the first time in my life, I feel a sense of wholeness, a sense that rightness is the chaos of order that the universe perversely attains with total ease. We, on the other hand, search in vain for the rightness of our point of view to impose our ownership of the world and god status on everyone and everything as though that will give credence to our lives and take the chaos into the order of our limited scope of awareness, thus attaining security and safety from what we cannot control.

I don't remember thinking to get a jacket before leaving the cabin, but the touch of her arm against mine gives me the feeling of warmth that you have facing a fire warmer than the rest and taking away the cold that could bite but doesn't. How is it that this doesn't feel cold? Instantly the answer comes from her, not as words, but as a total download of information. And now I know that the touch of her requests that my body generate as much warmth as it requires to be comfortable and that we have the ability to control what our bodies generate in warmth or cool, just for the asking. I think I'm liking this telepathic stuff. Then I think of one of those nights in the past and the sense that I was masturbating in the snow and she catches me and takes me and my body into the warmth of her being and the rush of orgasm molests my every morsel of sensate possibility with the expansiveness and growth of the connection to the entire universe.

Her laughter startles me out of my memory into the present and I suddenly feel a little embarrassed for having got caught, but the beauty of the laugh tinkling across the space mixes with the breeze in the trees as the snow slides from the needles of the pines in little splats of solidity that are like a dolphin breaking the surface of the ocean and sinking; there is no sound, only the ripples that show there is movement. Here too, there is movement as the snow falls, but I realize the movement is of the energy that the snow meeting the snow with a volume creates, and suddenly I know that same energy is what one feels with an avalanche, a flood and a falling rock. I now know what I have always been aware of without the words to describe.

I have felt the energy of things that were moving, like before an earthquake in California, I was restless and fidgety and awoke before it began and was standing outside in the darkness wondering what I was doing out there. I begin to understand the movements of energy before the physical sight, actually presents waves that give information if we will not give up our awareness. Strangest conversation I've never had with someone and boy, am I an uneducated slob.

She laughs again and the sheer delight of it caresses my body and my soul and I finally understand what caring without judgment does to embrace all the parts and pieces of you, and always I thought that this was what love would offer but never did. Again that odd sense of communication without words, and I realize it is the same energy of the snow falling into the snow. That when one thing that is, is falling into the oneness that is only to create an energy that ripples into the universe with great ease, silent assent to a new possibility, it becomes the choice for something more than our limited world can even imagine.

We move through the silent snow and I sense the water ahead as though it is breathing with the intensity of the rushing blood that one gets with exercise of the body that leaves exhilaration, sweat and throbbing awareness of every molecule and blood vessel and the sweet joy of tired and well-used muscles.

We walk up a small incline and the smell of the steam cantilevered against the cold and snow assaults my nose, the aromatic swell of volcanic mist and the extreme of the dry iciness of the snow and the blessed gift that it promises my body calls to every fiber of my body as the source for remembrance of the greatness of embodiment. That amazing feeling that there has always been more and that the promise is real and will be fulfilled.

As we top the rise, the mist from the springs meeting the cold air reminds me of those thick California fogs that leave the sounds of what isn't important to the sweet thickness of visceral silence that nurtures and cares for the moment only, neither the past nor the present are as willfully intense as the soundless sweetness that wraps and cleans the body and the mind with the sensorial closeness of presence with self.

She takes my hand and we move to the edge of the pool. We remove our clothes and put them on a rock that, obviously clear of snow and damp, promises to deliver warm clothes for our bodies at the end of our dip. We enter the water, its warmth and fragrance, the massive accumulation of miracles of years and thousands of plants and leaves boiled together as a brief stroke of sameness and togetherness and oneness of us all, the gift of earth to us and the gift that we are to the earth. Tears stream down my face at the realization of the travesties that man visits upon the earth and how she just gifts and gifts, never requiring return. The earth, which expands and nurtures us with the breath of air, takes our garbage and seldom rebels, the loving mother/father to all, and the source of some energy I can perceive like a call from the future of something I know, but cannot solidify to the simplicity of thought, and something that wishes from me, but doesn't demand, a call for possibility and a question of contribution that speaks only to the need to choose.

Please God, gods, powers that be, show me the way. The tears are followed by sobs, not for the earth, but for the sadness of mankind who has everything promised and refuses the golden gift and peace that this place is and could be across the face of the earth if we would but choose a reality that does not require destruction and is most enticing as that change. Oh blessed earth, can I now choose with you the true awareness that we are stewards for you and that choosing for you would be choosing for us.

We have been here for hours or weeks or minutes or forever, but the sense is that I finally know what I have been looking for my entire life and now I have found it. The “it” that I have found is me, the place of peace and joy and oneness with the entire universe that I be.

She takes my hand and leads me to my clothes and we sit on the rocks and the cold wraps me in her kindness and I do not feel the need of clothes, and yet Ruth begins to wrap me in the towel that has been there or just appeared and touches my body with her sweet hands, and the life and joy of being cared for and nurtured seems so right and real. My heart seems like it will leap from my breast to hers and that we will become one body with multiple parts entwined in each other, body and soul, and at that moment, I feel the sixty-seven join us and explode the limits of my brain and mind for the larger awareness that earth also nurtures and gifts to the union of our bodies and our beings for a possibility of what might be real and true that has never been experienced.

Chapter Twenty-Three

For three days I have remained alone, no food, no company, no Ruth, but the blessed oneness with all things has left me without a sense of need or a desire for anything.

The peace that I feel eliminates the desire or need of even food, and the sense that the entire world nurtures me and my body is greater than anything I have known before.

It is not yet dawn, the bright light of the moon permeates the landscape of my room and my soul and I choose the connection to Ruth that is no longer a necessity but a call for the desire I have known of her in the past.

I feel her in my mind and I know that she has requested my presence at the pool. I get out of bed, the moonlight all that I need to see the world, get dressed and leave that warmth of my room and the fire that has remained alive and banked for three days, no longer questioning how this is possible, just knowing that it is.

I arrive at the pool. The fog that silences all and wraps me in her tight nurturance stretches into the fiber of my body, my nostrils filled with molecules of water that float in the air like the pollens of summer, fragrant seductive, relaxing and intense with the fullness of the structures that now connect to every particle of my body and vibrate with the joy of being.

I know that she is here, I can sense her presence, and the mist moving and swirling serves as the catalyst for the memories of the past and the times that I have been here only in mind and totally in my soul.

As the mist lifts slightly in the breeze that softly moves about me, the chill of the air strokes my upper body exposed from the intense warmth of the water and the goose pimples invigorate and inspire my body to more sensation that I have known was possible. She is here facing me across the pool. The water just above her breasts hides what I now intensely desire. I feel her touch of being in my body and I reach out with my being to touch her body. I can feel what her body is sensing and the goose pimples of my chest create matching goose pimples on her nipples and I feel my body feeling her body and her feeling me and mine and we are entwined in the molecular structure of one another. The intimacy that this brings and the spring of life to loins with each other and the molecules clanging together as the space that is us experiences the movement of the solidity of bodies, is the expression of desire for life that we futilely call lust. I smell her hair in the dew of the fog, and the wetness of her hair and the drift of her scent stimulate more dynamically the need of her body next to mine.

I close my eyes and start to remember what it was like in my dreams, and as I do, the past memory robs the heat of the moment and she begins to withdraw from my body. I have withdrawn from her in the moments of bringing the fantasies of the past to the sexual moment of now. I open my eyes and am once again entwined with her body and being and the arousal of hers and mine is bringing me to the brink of what I would call orgasm, and suddenly she expands my awareness and we are in a bigger pool with greater distance between us physically and that intensity of feeling, her feeling me begins to bring my body and hers back to the boil point. Just as I wish to explode, I hear her wish for expansion. And I do.

Once again that sense that her body is further away is belied by the smell of her hair and body and the movement towards me and the rise of those amazing breasts above the water, the nipples hard from the cold that is mine, I sink into the water and the need of explosion goes to something that is more intimate in the awareness of her caring and that feeds the part of me that I found three days before.

The need to touch her and her willingness to touch me expands again, like the forest and the animals who embrace the gift of life, we become that gift of life to each other and to the world and once again I reach for the being that she is, that is also me and our bodies respond with an orgasm that is riotous and raucous in the incredible peace and expansion of it. This is what the Buddhists must mean by the inner orgasm.

Once again we expand, and in doing so our bodies move without effort or muscle towards each other, we are driven and required to touch, and the moment she reaches and touches my hand I experience again that orgasmic quality of sensitivity that sends waves through my body and hers.

I touch her and the slightest of touches sends off an explosive demand of more within my body and she has not touched me. I lean forward and press my lips gently to hers. I feel my beard as the stubble electrifies her body and the touch of our tongues, but a butterfly touch, sends shocks to my very toes and the warmth that increases in our crotch, not crotches, for we seem now to be one body with four arms and legs and one torso suggesting to the other what next to do. We sink into the hot water knowing that the heat of our bodies now expands the heat of the water and that the water is one with our body and the joy of it is also the joy of us.

We slowly and with great care bring our body to itself and the place of it within itself sliding with the water and with the steam and with the fog and the cold sensitizes every part and piece with the sensorial dynamism of ever-expanding waves of sensation, intensity, perverse satisfaction and stupefying possibilities, and the shadows of the future embrace the value of the moment with the alteration of time and space into the caress of movement together as one.

As the dawn arrives, so do we. We come together, the earthquake that comes with the ejaculation of my body into hers, and her ejaculation into my body rocks the foundation of my life and my sexual experience with the beauty and the joy of light and space and the song of the birds, which commences at the exact moment of us being the body of life together. The orchestration of these moments and the space of life that we all are together includes all and deletes nothing. She kisses me briefly, fleetingly the sensation producing another orgasm in our body. I look into the face of the woman I have known forever and for only a moment and hold her in my arms hoping for it to last forever and again we are racked with waves of orgasms that are like that aftershocks of the earthquake that is us.

We walk from the pool and across the snow, the cold creating another orgasm as our bodies respond to yet another stimulus. I wonder if life is truly an ongoing orgasm that we usually refuse, but that thought is replaced by the awareness of the day's activity that Ruth places in my head. I open the cabin door and a roaring fire greets us as does the sweet bed I love as much as her.

"Thanks, Jacob, for being everything that you are."

Chapter Twenty-Four

It's almost Christmas. For three months now Ruth and I have been together, and the time has flown like the days have had a living, breathing, joyful exuberance, that like us have no beginning and no end. Conversation is unnecessary, possibilities increase every day and the life we live has so much in every moment that the needs of the outside world cease.

Our lives intertwine with the orgasmic joy of living that is like the pools in which we made first physical love. Those pools are like the sexual union we now experience.

The first is the big pool in which we feel healed, and waters expand with the seasons of the year. The second pool is hotter, and like our sexual appetite, is deeper and hotter and nurturing as its gift. The third pool is hotter yet, and as we expand our own capacity for more intensity, we experience a level of caring that the earth gifts to us and that we gift to the earth. The fourth pool is hotter and tighter and requires that that we be more creative and move with the currents and the possibility of what is next. The fifth pool requires a sense of joy, joy in the heat and the passion of the extremes of the body sensing what can only be described as a greater will to experience the molecular peace of communion that creates joy. The sixth pool is the one that is bigger and slower and hotter yet and descries the necessity of expanding both body and being in order to know what is truly possible to experience. The seventh pool is the most intense and is the source of being one with the universe to actually embrace what is possible and with that immenseness, the orgasm of life begins, but does not end.

This has been my daily experience of living with Ruth. Not being in the pools but experiencing everything the pools represent with each meeting and joining of our bodies.

How great is life now that these are the dynamic moments of each day and each experience. I would wish to give her everything and yet there is the awareness that when you can live forever, little has much value in the holding of it only in the knowing of it.

The door begins to open and I am aware of "her" coming to see me.

"Hello, Ruth. I was just thinking about Christmas and giving gifts. Do you do that in this place?"

I suddenly get the answer directly without the limitations of language, and I have the whole of how the real Christmas in "the place" is more about the energies that we gift to the earth on that day and that we will not have the trees and the ornaments and the food that is part of the world I came from and which I have so little desire to return for.

"Jacob, the boys do have a gift for you, but since we do not do gifts, you can have it now, and the boys would be so happy if they could give it to you now."

Suddenly the boys are in the room. The delight on their faces is infectious and I begin to laugh and that instills great joy and laughter in their worlds as well as Ruth's.

"Mr. Rayne, will you come with us to the barn now?" It's so odd when they talk in unison. Mostly because when they think at you, it is so much easier to recognize which is which.

As we walk towards the barn, a sense of elation that makes little sense to me, I suddenly recognize as their elation. I now know that this is more special than what I have had presented to me in the past months and that seemed so extraordinary, the fact that this is unique for them is exciting.

They open the barn door and there in the subdued light of the very old barn is the beauty and joy of my life, my sweet T-bird, and she is shinier and more pristine than when I drove her all those months ago, before the deer.

The tears begin to roll down my face at the amazing difference she is, for indeed she is better than I have ever known her to be.

"Boys, how did you do this? She is like a brand new car."

"Well, Mr. Rayne, we just asked the molecules to return to what they originally were, and we had the pictures from you of what she was all about and so we asked for that to show up for us."

"What do you mean, you asked?" I have that odd feeling again that I am being educated in quantum physics when I am still in kindergarten.

"Well, one of the things we have learned in 'the place' is that even the molecules have a consciousness of their own and when you request in just the right... I guess you would call it, the right vibration… that's not really all it is, but sort of, then the molecules can change or become what you ask of them."

"Thanks, boys, that's as clear as mud to me, but I am truly grateful to see her looking so beautiful."

"Mr. Rayne, we have a problem. Her lights don't work and she won't roar anymore. We couldn't get her to do that for us."

I remember her being on her back and I realize that there may be a good reason for the problems. I open the hood and look at the battery, it looks good until I open it up and discover that all the acid must have leaked out and most likely that means the gas is all gone as well.

As they read my mind, the boys suddenly grasp all of it, the whole concept of how this works. "Guys, how did you get her here? I haven't seen any roads that lead here, only pathways."

"Well, you know how we appear and disappear? That's how we got you and her here, it's not hard when there are two of us and we do it better than anyone else."

"Thanks, guys, I have to get a battery for her and some gasoline, where can I get those?"

"There's a small town about thirty miles from here and we have a friend there who will help us, but we don't have any money, and you don't have much either, we looked in your wallet when we found you. Do you want to go meet him now?"

My answer only thought and received, they touch my hands, and we are now outside of a small town that appears to be basically empty. The wide concrete streets are reminders of the twenties when everything seemed to be about space, except the people. The storefronts along the street are silent and empty like the shadows of the past, left to remind us that someone or something has been before, and it, too, has disappeared.

There seem to be a few cars parked in front of a general store, gas station, and eatery all rolled into one.

The boys and I begin to walk towards the store. It seems odd to be back in civilization, if you can call this civilization, after all the months of quiet and solitude, and I recognize that what I had called solitude was extremely full of awareness and moment-by-moment presence, and that civilization doesn't have that, it sort of seems empty and missing. Missing what I am not sure, but definitely something is missing. Maybe it's just the fact that the town is basically deserted. The snow piled up along the sidewalks leaves no doubt that few walk these streets, and the snowplow just moves the snow away from the street and allows the cars to pass. It's a little odd that the snow seems to be clean and drifted, not blown out of the filth of the road. The side streets with the boarded-up houses and the two-foot layer of snow attest to the idea that few come here and perhaps even fewer live here.

We enter the store, and a nice looking man moves around the counter smiling. "Hi boys, how are you? And you must be Jacob." I know that I am supposed to be used to the odd things that happen around the boys, but I didn't expect this. "My name is Ryan Boyle, and the lovely lady coming out of the back there is my wife Lulah May." He laughs and I know that he is reading my thoughts, "Oh my God, these can't be the Lulah May and Ryan from Uncle Jed's story." She laughs in the soft musical tones that remind me of Stormy, and I know with certainty that these are the same folks. They look older than the rest of the clan. "Jacob, how about a cup of coffee?" He leads us into the restaurant part of the store and we sit. No one else seems to be around.

"Yes, Jacob, we look older, because we have lived here since the twenties. This was a boomtown in the early 1900s, gold and silver were found here and the town grew. The silver and gold petered out in the thirties and everyone started drifting away. As a group, we realized that having some connection with the outside world would be useful to the seekers, and you would be amazed at how many of them show up here looking for maps or food or lodging, and we make sure they realize and find what they are truly looking for.

"I gather you need a battery and some gas. 'She' has escaped the boys' knowledge of change and now a little science of the old fashioned kind is required."

"Let's try your credit cards and see what happens."

Oddly, I feel like he knows what's going to happen and I feel that something is not right with my financial world at all.

As Ryan calls for the battery, I pull my wallet from my pants, the first time I have had it out in months, I wonder if moths will fly out when I open it. I take out my credit card and he reads it to the man at the store for batteries. He doesn't look even vaguely surprised when it is declined and I pull out my ATM card and give him that, knowing that it has at least fifty thousand available, and it is declined. He thanks the man and hangs up the phone. "Perhaps you should call your wife and find out what has happened."

With the leaden feeling I had through most of my years of marriage, that sense of impending doom that bloomed on the horizon daily like a lightning storm that has not yet stabbed its disaster to ground but growls constantly before striking, I pick up the phone and dial.

She answers. "Patty, this is Jacob."

"Jacob, you are alive, I have been so worried, and Stevie cried for days about you and then he said you started visiting him every night and had told him you were coming soon and would take him someplace if he would like to go. And I couldn't believe you were still alive, where have you been and why haven't you called, you are so inconsiderate of others."

"Patty, I was in an automobile accident and haven't been able to call. And what happened to my credit cards and the money in my ATM? Why don't these work?"

"Jacob, don't take that testy tone with me, you know how much I hate that. Besides, when you didn't call after six weeks and we hadn't heard from you, I thought maybe you had been killed or kidnapped or you had finally been taken up by aliens, hehe, so I contacted the bank and your credit cards. You had forgotten to take me off as beneficiary, so I told them to cancel the cards until further notice and said that since Stevie was your beneficiary and you owed me alimony and child support, I got them to turn everything over to me, so there isn't anything left in your name for anybody to steal. I think I was brilliant to take care of everything you forgot, don't you?"

"Patty I need a new battery for my car, otherwise I can't get home."

"Well, you should have thought of that before you stopped calling. Didn't you realize how that would worry me? But the good news is that because I realized how much I missed you, I know that we can put our marriage back together, because I no longer think I don't care. Isn't that wonderful?"

"Can I use one of your credit cards to buy the battery?"

"You know, I would have to ask my attorney about that, before I could let that occur, if you call in a couple of days, I will have time to get to him and get his recommendation, okay?"

"Okay Patty, we'll talk soon, bye."

The looks on Ryan's and Lulah May's faces, bemused laughter suppressed, relieves some of the anger I feel so strongly.

Lulah May laughs softly. "Nice to know there is someone who truly cares about you out there."

And with that I begin to laugh, half hysteria, half relief and total amusement at the insanity that I have half returned to with one telephone call. Now I understand those knowing looks that came before the credit card fiasco. "You knew, you bastards, you knew." The tears, the laughter, and the intense joy at realizing I have Ruth and the boys and the rest of those in "the place" washes away the years of repeated strangeness that I thought constituted normal marriage. I know that I am free of the illusion, which I have lived, breathed, and called true for me, and I know that love will not conquer all and that beauty does not will out and that giving 150 percent will only give you someone who will take 200 percent and all your money. The joy I feel in every pore of body and soul sends a shiver of gratitude for the gift that insane little conversation has given me.

"Now what do I do, Ryan?"

"Jacob, you remember the story about Uncle Jed finding gold when he was back East? Have you ever considered how he did that?"

"To be honest, I assumed he had some machine or divining rods or something that led him to the gold."

"Boys, will you take this vial of gold nuggets and Jacob and lead him to the creek around Devlin's point. Show him how to ask the gold to come to him."

The boys touch my hands, and suddenly we are by a small creek, and I can only assume by the fact that there is a tall rock that looks like a point, that we have arrived. "Now what, boys?"

"Okay, Mr. Rayne. This is how you do it. You know how you can feel the difference in us when you close your eyes? Well, this isn't really any different. The group knew you would have this ability when you could tell the difference between us with such ease and the fact that you could feel the numbers of people in "the place" instantaneously. So what we want you to do is place the gold in one hand and then the other until you have the feeling of the difference between with and without. To help, we have an identical bottle filled with just sand. Close your eyes and we will move the bottles back and forth."

As the bottles began to move back and forth from one hand to the other, I suddenly can feel the energetic difference that the gold had. "Boys, I've got it. I can feel the difference."

The boys walk towards the stream, the snow, a bundle of protection for the ground, disappears in a twelve foot circle as the boys touch it; it just sort of slides away from their hands.

"Okay Mr. Rayne, now you have to ask for the gold to come to you, just the way you called for us that first night when you were hurt."

"I don't remember what that was like, boys." Suddenly their thoughts invade my mind, and I can feel the intensity of how they must have felt my thoughts that night. It is so demanding and commanding, with an added passion of need, I kind of hate the awareness of how it sounded. The boys laugh and the embarrassment that I feel leaves almost instantly.

"That's exactly the energy that you have to use to call the gold to you, Mr. Rayne, just ask and you will receive."

I bend down and sort of squat over the cold, bare earth that moments before had been covered with snow. As my hands begin to sweep over the ground, it is as though they have developed a life of their own, I remember the night of the accident and that energy of "need" that brought the boys, and as they disappear, I feel a tug on the palm of my hand and I stop and increase that feeling of "need and tug" and the sand beneath my hand begins to shake and vibrate like something alive is digging its way out. Suddenly the tug on the palm ceases, and as I look down, there is a small gold nugget under my hand. I start to yell with joy just as the boys reappear. They have a box with them, wood, old and sturdy by anyone's standard, and they jump up and down and cheer too. I get the distinct impression that I am the child who has just learned to ride a two-wheeler and they are the parent who is proud and shocked that it came so easily.

I have spent three days totally entranced with "need and tug," and I have most of my box filled with small chunks of gold and flakes of it as well. I have had more fun doing this from dawn to dusk than any time in my life. Interesting that it doesn't seem to be because it is money, but rather the playing with the energy, the way a small child builds a sand castle, not to complete anything, but just for the sheer joy of generating something from nothing and standing back with pride at the accomplishment of it all.

Thank God, the boys have come each night, and Lulah May has given me a warm bowl of soup and a comfy bed. It seems odd that I have eaten nothing for these three days but the soup, and I feel not so much sleepy each night but contented. Odd that the needs I had always had in my life before seem irrelevant when what I am having to "eat" is the energy of the earth and the cold and the wind and the sun, pale as it is, and nothing makes me tired, just grateful for the blessing, a gift, that the earth does provide upon request.

Each moment seems like an eternity and "need and tug" works easier and better every time I use it. The flakes of gold that come to the surface are easy to get up once I figure out that being the energy of the gold and asking it creates a force field or something that makes it adhere to my skin until I reverse the flow and it all falls in the box. I have spent the last two hours using the energy, but haven't gotten a single tug anywhere, and even as I try the snow further away, there is no "call" of the gold to my hand or my hands to it.

The boys appear, as they have each evening when I get tired or frustrated, odd how they always know, and wonderful. Cell phones would definitely be less than valuable here, and the psychic towers can't be stopped by mountains or dead zones. "Okay Mr. Rayne, you have apparently mined this area clean. We will take the box back to Uncle Ryan and return for you."

They disappear, and I sit on the rock that offers itself for rest, and the cold creeps into my awareness and the sun hides its beautiful face behind the darkening clouds, which speak of snow, and suddenly I realize these truly are snow clouds, and I can feel the amount, the length of the storm, the depth of snow and all the elements around me talking. The very molecules of the air gift their own consciousness and speak a language that I now have as a new and greater awareness of the contribution the world is to us, always has been, and yet has only been understood by sages and sirens and shamans in the rest of the world. How full the world and my life feel.

The boys appear, touch my hands and once again we are outside the town.

"Why are we having to walk so far, guys? I like it better when you put me in front of the potbelly stove."

"There are couple of seekers in the store today, so we have to be totally normal and civilized, and Aunt Lulah May said for you to be quiet about what you been doing. She opened one of the houses on the side street and has mentioned that a few people live here in town, mostly during the summer, so that they won't ask about your car or why you are walking. We will be staying with you tonight in the other house, we are your nephews. Can you remember all that?"

The obvious joy the boys are having over this subterfuge makes me laugh and I let them know telepathically that I get it.

"We can't do that thought stuff tonight, 'cause that freaks the new ones out, so don't do that, Uncle Jacob. And from now on you are another uncle, okay?"

"Yes, boys, I get it. I think I can do this, and I will do my best."

As we enter the store, Ryan gets up and comes toward us from the stove. "Jacob, come on in and warm yourself, the weatherman says we're going to get quite a storm." And he winks. I guess that means I'm the weatherman.

"Ryan, what's that smell, I think I smell? Lulah May's famous soup? Does she have enough for me and the boys?"

"I think she made enough for some unknown army that arrives some time tonight." He laughs, and then tells me with his mind to watch the seekers.

I walk over to the stove and there are two men and a woman in their thirties. They look a little worn and care filled. The woman is probably younger, her long blonde hair is a little greasy, like it hasn't been washed for a while. One of the men is a sandy brown long-haired hippie-looking guy and the other is a black-haired man with dark skin who looks like he is part black and has the most startling blue eyes I have ever seen, let alone from someone with his apparent ethnic background. They look warily at me, and the boys, and I can feel the thoughts in their heads. They are feeling extremely strange, they don't know why they are here and they wish that they could get a hold of some drugs or alcohol so they could have more of a sense of comfort. I walk over and extend my hand to the blue-eyed one. "Hi, I'm Jacob Rayne, and these are my nephews Rob and Roy, they only look like twins." The joke breaks the tension and the three relax a little. "How did you find this place and come to stop here?"

Blue Eyes, leans forward and smiles, the sweet soul that the eyes hinted at breaks through with one of the most amazing smiles I have ever seen. This young man should have been a model or actor, with this kind of beauty. "Mr. Rayne, you're funny, and I am Alex, this is Charlie and the pretty blonde girl is his secret love, Blossom."

"Alex, I think you're funny, too, because the energy that runs between those two is so intense I don't think it's a very well-kept secret."

Blossom smiles and the energy of affection and caring between her and Charlie increases by three, and obviously she is grateful that there is no longer a need for secret. I wonder what is really going on for these three.

"Would you three like to join me and my nephews for dinner? It's simple fare, but Lulah May is the best cook in a hundred miles, so you don't want to miss it."

"Mr. Rayne, we wouldn't want to impose or interfere with your family time," Alex says, but I know from what's in his head that this is not actually the case, he just can't believe that a stranger would ask them.

"Alex, Charlie, Blossom, the boys and I would be honored to have your company for dinner, you might have to put up with Lulah May and Ryan as well, but we promise to be on our best behavior and not scare you with wild stories of ghosts and spirits haunting our little village."

Their laughter was all the answer that was needed, and Lulah May brought out the plates and cutlery for a nice meal. The smell of baking bread brought taste buds to life and we chatted aimlessly for about an hour until dinner was served.

"You all didn't tell us how you ended up coming to this deserted corner of the universe," said Ryan.

For way too many seconds, the silence pervaded before Alex spoke. "We had actually been arguing for the last two hours of our drive. Blossom and Charlie want to settle down and try to live normal lives and think that all they have done for the last fifteen years is not normal, and that marriage and children will solve the feeling of not belonging that has plagued all of us since we were teenagers. And I was railing about that not ever working and how you don't change a leopard's spots and then we fell silent for about ten minutes before we saw the sign that said "Needful, the town you seek," and we turned without a word and found ourselves here. I know that it sounds strange, but it just felt right, and Charlie, Mr. Normal, was the guy driving."

I see by the energy that swirls around these people that they are everything I was before I came here, and my heart swells with a desire to show them and the need to be quiet. Ryan thinks, "Not now Jake" and I realize that all those months ago they let me take my time, and it worked, so obviously they know how to give people the clues they need to get their own awareness.

As Lulah May rises to clear the table she says, "Jake, could you put Alex up for the night? I only have one room that would be good for Charlie and Blossom, and you have that extra room over at your place. Maybe the boys could go light the fireplaces and get the place warm enough for our visitors from the south." She just did it, nothing had been mentioned about them being from southern California, she just dropped it in, in such a way that they would be questioning whether they or their license plate had indicated it or whether something else had occurred. I am impressed with that, I wonder if I will be able to be that slick when it is my turn. "Lulah May, yes that's a good idea, Alex and we boys at the bachelor pad. Can we come for breakfast in the morning?"

"Of, course, Jake, we will have some stuff ready by eight."

"Jake" says Ryan, "can I talk to you just a moment, on the porch about your box that we were researching?"

"Sure, Ryan." We go out to the front porch, the silence roaring with the peace and space of glowing whiteness. "Jake, I did some reckoning on the value of the gold you found. You have just under two hundred thousand right now."

I laugh so loud that I swear the snow stops and listens for the break in peace that this laugh is to it. "Well, I guess I have enough to get my car going."

"I think you might be better off than you were before, what do you think Jake? By the way, how about you let me bank it for you a little at a time so that the IRS doesn't take notice and neither does your ex-wife, and we'll set it up so no one but you can get their mitts on it, sound good?"

Interesting, in the past I would have had the paranoid point of view that I had to keep total control of that much money, but when the earth gives it with such ease and abundance, it no longer seems like a relevant or real point of view. "Sounds perfect, Ryan, thanks."

"We better go back in now and see how the troops are doing."

As Ryan and I slip back into the warmth of the store, the boys are telling Alex that if he is good, they will get Uncle Jake to tell him a really cool bedtime story that will excite him and make him happy. The mind connection tells me the story I will be telling will be mine. Am I ready for this?

Chapter Twenty-Five

A half hour later, Alex and I are leaving the store, the boys have gone ahead to light the fires, like they actually needed to be there to do it. As we walk through the gently falling snowflakes, the crunch of our shoes the only context to actually being on planet earth, Alex takes a deep breath and sighs, the silence, raw testament to the lack of peace in this kind man's life and mind.

As we enter the house, the boys send me the message of how to tell my story, not as a biography, but as a possible plot for a novel.

"Alex, the boys promised you a story, so if you don't mind sitting in the rocker in their room while I tell the story, then you are welcome to join us, or I can show you your room and give you a good book to read."

"Jacob, I think I would like to listen to the story, my dad used to tell me stories about the days after the Nazis in Germany and how tough it was. Bedtime stories were always about things that should have been true and sometimes were true. My father was German and my mother was a nurse. My father was born in the U.S. in the fifties, but his parents wanted to make sure that no one ever forgot what happened with the Nazis, and the suffering that Germany experienced after they lost. My mother's family was from the south and they moved to California to get clear of the prejudice that created the civil rights movement. I was born during their hippie love days, and my first name is actually Dylan, but it is so hippie generation that I use my middle name so I don't have to put up with the grief."

Odd how this young man just gave me everything I could have asked in one short conversation. I look at the boys and the smiles indicate that they have been playing with his mind. I think back at them that they better keep it clean. The smiles widen. No such luck.

"Well, Alex, tonight's story is the idea I have had for a novel or a screenplay, and I don't know how I should do this. The boys have already heard the beginning. Boys, should I start where we left off, or should I bring Alex up to date?"

"Uncle Jake, we loved the part you told last night. How about doing it again and you can fill in some of the details, and that way Alex won't feel left out and we get to enjoy it too," says Rob.

I begin to tell what had happened to me at the beginning. I tell it in the third person as though I was standing outside myself and not really involved in the circumstances. I tell the story for about an hour and then the boys appear to be asleep and I suggest we sneak out of the room. Telepathically the boys have told me that is enough for this seeker tonight.

"Well, Alex, I guess you have got to be tired, so I'll let you go to bed."

"Actually, Jake, could we just chat for a while? Your story kind of stirred a few things for me."

"Sure Alex, what would you like to talk about?"

"Well, my whole life I've felt that there had to be a place like the one you described, and I've always felt that the things you described about people with 'powers' for lack of words, should actually exist. Do you believe in this kind of stuff, is that how you created the story?"

"I definitely believe in what I have described to you and more than that, I have had a few experiences like deja vu and telepathic awareness that parallel my story. Do I expect others to believe? No, I just have always known that there had to be more in the world or there didn't seem to be much reason to continue to live."

"Jake, that's the way I feel. I've been planning my death for the last six months because I just can't seem to find anything that brings me a sense of joy and happiness, and the description you had for the main character and his marriage and the hopelessness are all too real to me, it is my life. One of the reasons that Charlie and I were arguing on the way here was because he is expecting Blossom to be the source of the happiness he can never find, any more than I can, and I told him that that is too much of a burden to place on Blossom and children. How can anyone other than you make you happy?"

"Alex, I get the point and I agree. The reality for me is that I have found everything I have been looking for my whole life and it is right here if you only ask."

"Jake, on that note, I think bed is a good idea."

Chapter Twenty-Six

The next day passed with the snow stranding the seekers in town, they didn't seem to mind. We had breakfast and lunch and I watched in wonder as Ryan and Lulah May dropped bombs into their universe and also in memory of the way in which the concepts of "the place" were laid at my feet and then I had to pick up the pieces and assimilate into them and the people.

As night descends and the snow shrouds us in its gentle silence, the boys take Alex's hands and begin to lead him towards the house. I wonder what they are doing to him energetically, because he begins to weave as though the single glass of wine and all the water have made him drunk. Poor guy, he has no idea. But then I remember being that poor guy a few short months ago, or perhaps it has been a few hundred years.

As we enter the house, the fires are roaring and the house is warm to a degree that almost necessitates stripping down. I laugh as Alex tries to reason logically how this is possible when he has been sitting with the boys and me for the last two hours, but either he has made it logical or he is accepting already what it took me weeks to fathom. Of course, I was older and far more cynical by nature than Alex.

The boys rush for bed and Alex follows, glancing back to see if I am coming, I can almost feel his mind connect with mine and then he breaks the connection and moves on up the stairs to the room that may seal his fate.

I love it when I get all dramatic and think that a great significance is occurring when perhaps it is just a snowflake falling again.

I sit in the chair and begin to describe the moments of realizing that I have been here before and that I know this person whose name is Ruth, and I talk about the knowing of each other and the presence and the gift of desire and possibility and realizing that there is someone in the world who can embrace my being and welcome me into her life as though we have always been together. As I finish this story and the twins are pretending to be totally asleep, especially for the sex scenes, which they were totally a part of in the beginning. I look over to Alex to ask him to leave the room and I watch for several minutes as the man cries silently, and the tears fall from his chin like the rain falls from the leaves, without rancor or need, but from something that is perhaps greater, a sense that what is, can become.

We leave the room, a silent awareness of the needs of youth, or so we would tell ourselves, to justify the level of perception that has just occurred and is occurring. The tears keep coming and Alex seems not embarrassed, but actually relieved.

“So what’s happening Alex?”

“Jake, you just described what I have been searching for, for the last six years of my life. That dream you talked about, well every night for the last six years I have been searching in my dreams for the girl called Jessie, who always invites me home, though I never quite get where home is, and I look for the black hair and blue eyes, that make mine seem lifeless and lackluster by comparison, and I feel the pools and the sensations and I wake up every morning expecting to be someplace where she is and I always want to go back to sleep so that I can do it again. Six years of wet dreams and no reality. Just to know that someone else has that point of view and that it might actually come together is the best thing I‘ve heard in years, and I feel somehow validated in a way that makes no sense to me at all. But I want you to know that these two evenings and the story you are creating are like hearing about what I know has to exist that no other person in the world has ever stated as either possible or even vaguely true as a possibility. I hope you will let me gift you my undying gratitude for the peace that just knowing one other person in the world has a willingness to believe that what is real to me might actually be real. Thanks.”

With that, he goes to bed, and I begin to feel that something very important has taken place tonight and that this man will actually be joining our group in a very short period of time. I wonder how the others feel, and suddenly I know how the sixty-seven are getting this, and they let me know that tomorrow will change his life and mine.

Chapter Twenty-Seven

Morning, and the snow has ended. The silence and the quiet are profoundly comforting. I dress for the cold of the day that is to come. It's odd how now I am always prepared for what is to happen each day at the moment of waking. When you function from the awareness of all that is around you at all times, there is no accident, and at the same time the fullness of each moment and each day is also the continuing, expansive joy of exploration. I look out the window and the main street looks to have been plowed, but not having heard a machine and knowing the capacities of the group, I realize that they somehow have invited the snow to move, much the same as I have invited the gold to visit.

The boys are suddenly by my side, and they grab my hands and we are suddenly a short distance outside of town. There is my sweet T-bird, and a pretty girl with jet-black hair and blue, blue eyes sits in the passenger seat of the running car. As I walk up to the driver's side, the running car purrs like the tiger in its tank that I so love, and heat emanates from the car with a level of intensity she never had before. The girl extends her hand and states, "Hi, Jake, I'm Jessica."

Holy shit, now I understand what the sixty-seven meant when they said today would change Alex. God knows, I just got changed. I realize that this beautiful girl looks like Norma Lea, and as she reads my mind her laughter is exactly like her mother's. I feel hugely joyful, as I feel the life that Alex is about to have.

The boys disappear and I feel them wake Alex and move him towards the windows to check the out-of-doors. I have mentioned the car in my "story," and as I drive towards the house, the snow disappears along the street where "I live." We drive to the front of the house, the door opens and Alex races out of the house, bare feet and boxers, the cold not even possible in his world as he runs to the car, and Jessie stands and embraces him with a caress of being that is so very intimate and joyful that I want to turn aside and not watch and cannot, and I know that there is no way not to know how they feel and the thoughts they are sharing with a level of presence that took me months to achieve. He lifts her out of the car and moves away from the car, the boys and me, and into the house that will be their refuge for the next several months.

"Well, boys, do you think that everything will be okay with them for now and that we will eventually see them?"

The giggles that come from them and the sparkle of their eyes are affirmation that they are seeing and hearing things even I cannot.

We get in the car, and I drive the boys to the general store, the delight in their world gives me the same elation that I had the day they gave me back my car. Ryan and Lulah May are there with Blossom and Charlie, standing on the porch, having watched half of the exchange. Their thoughts are like reading a book with huge letters and they both have seen the girl, Jessie, and apparently Alex has talked with them a great deal, with great detail, so they now know what has occurred. Ryan lets me know that they have given the details of their needs and they have talked all night long about "the place" and they, too, know what is really true and possible and will leave the needs of normal for the gift that they can now be. My world feels like it has expanded 300 percent as a result of these three adding themselves to this band of people who populate "the place."

My awareness has grown in some strange way I cannot describe, and suddenly I can hear my son crying and the anger that his mother is delivering at him that has nothing to do with him, and I realize I must now leave and return to him so that he will live and survive.

Ruth's thoughts fill me with the invitation to return to her. I so don't wish to leave and yet I know that I must. There is no sense of rejection or blame or even wrongness that what is, is what is for me. She is her amazing kindness and gifting for me and her and the group and "the place."

I hate that I must leave, but I know that I must, for me at least the obligation you take on when you have children requires a constancy of contribution without end and without rancor. I begin to pray that his mother will somehow let me have him and the horror of what I have to do or say that might get her to change is like a fire that dies from the bottom up as the flood comes into a house from below. It just begins to fizzle and die without a hope that wind or wood or paper will keep it alive. Suddenly from every member of "the place," including the new arrivals, I feel the support of possibilities that shred the willingness to fail in favor of the knowing that all things can be changed if you are willing to live from the joy that the earth and the universe gift, and regardless of what happens, there will be something that will lead to something that is greater than what our experience can claim as truth in favor of the universe, which gifts what we ask if we but have the courage to ask.

I park the car in the shed next to the store that used to be a garage for mechanics and walk with the boys to the store.

Ryan and Lulah May smile those same annoying, knowing smiles that tell they have it all, and they send to me the information that I have to go to Ruth now, to say goodbye. The boys take my hands and we melt from needful into "the place." The whole clan is there, each sending me the peace of caring and the awareness that they, too, always know what they have to do when they have to do it.

Ruth takes my hand and we begin to walk towards the pools, and the thoughts that pass between us are more rapid and complete and generous in their possibilities than I have ever known was possible. I know that I shall miss these kinds of moments and at the same moment, I also realize that that is not really possible. The truth is that this kind of connection transcends all time and space, and gifts to those that receive with total ease whenever they have need. Sort of like a psychic "need and tug" for the soul.

Chapter Twenty-Eight

We spend the day walking through the woods enjoying the sun and the crisp air of winter, and now we have come back to my little cabin. The fire is roaring and the bed is ready for us. I know and she knows that this will be the last night we may have together, oh God, can it last forever?

She lays down on the bed, her clothes slip away from her body with the invisible hands of my request. My clothes fall to ground and I step out of them at her request. I sit on the bed next to her, and wishing to fill myself with every fiber of her being, I begin to put my hands over her body and to touch the energy that is her. The intense desire to have her within me not just my body leaves an ache that I cannot explain. About an inch above her body, I begin to touch and stroke the energy of her and the darkness of the room changes as the electric arc of tiny lightning bolts spear from her body to my hand and the electricity excites the electricity of my body with a longing to own that sweet spark of life within me and my body. The electric sparks arcing in the dark leave a blue hue to air around us, and we both feel the desire to bring our bodies together and to have again that communion of total orgasm that is greater than body and more than earth. I continue to stroke over her whole body and the lightning becomes a greater and greater turn-on, and our bodies begin to vibrate with a rhythm of their very own. The demand and need to put our bodies together arises and flushes out the moments that linger and expand. Tiny orgasms rock her body as the "need and tug" brings stronger bolts of electricity from her body to mine. We have been at this for nearly an hour and the electricity gives more and more connection of the two of us as though we are nothing but the accumulation of thousands of atomic fusions coming together to expand our energies and our body.

Finally, neither of us can wait longer, I rise over her body and as I begin to lower towards her succulent spaciousness that I have not even touched, a lightning bolt springs from the entirety of my body and caresses her whole body with a fire storm that rages from one end of us to the other and I enter her and explode with an orgasm that takes us both to the other end of the universe and back, and we scream with—and are in sync with—the wolves and coyotes and the birds of the night and every living breathing rock and tree and snowflake within the world.

Chapter Twenty-Nine

It's morning, and the boys have come and taken me and Ruth to the general store and my car. We climb the stairs to the store, my heart both full and devastated with the longing for what I must leave, and the caring that she gives takes the longing away only to have it increase tenfold.

Ryan comes towards me with a package. "Here is twenty thousand of the money you have, don't worry, you can't be mugged when you are aware and can hear everyone's thoughts. We will see you sooner than you think and "the place" will call you when it is time for you to return. There's some food in here, too, which Lulah May thinks will make you happy. Don't be concerned, my friend, you know about "need and tug" and that will always come to the rescue." The lascivious smile on the faces of the crowd brings laughter to my soul. How strange it is to know that there are no secrets or secret moments from these wonderful people.

Alex and Jessie enter the store. I see by the look on their faces that they, too, enjoyed my moments from the night before.

"Jake, thanks for the learning last night. Your bedtime story, yeah, I get it was a setup, was helpful in moving into the fun of last night. Apparently, we are not the only ones who where lucky enough to enjoy last night."

The laughter in the group is reassuring, like when you have friends who enjoy a raunchy joke, but this is even greater.

I know it is time to go. I turn without goodbye, for there is no ending when you have this kind of connection, and walk to the car. It starts with the beauty of newness and the door shuts gently and sweetly. I back out of the garage and turn to leave down the road to where I don't belong, away from everything that has given me, me.

As I drive past the store, the group all wave, not the wave of goodbye, farewell, but rather the sense is that all will be greater in the going. Ruth has no tears, just that sweet joyful serenity that nurtured my soul since the very first time I met her.

As I drive through the softness of the new snowfall and watch as the needles in the pines sift sprinkles of icy beauty upon the drifts below, I feel the gift of Ruth and the others and "the place" connecting me to everything I have become and everything I am that I had always missed before coming here. I know I will never forget, and I will see this as the time I found me and the possibilities of everything in the world being part of my life from now on. "Goodbye, sweet people, thank you for the gifts you have given me. The gift of you and of what is really possible in life and more than that the gift of me."

Chapter Thirty

Ruth stands on the porch as Jacob leaves, a smile wisps across her face as she feels his goodbye. Her hand rests on her belly and she rubs it gently. "Thanks Jacob, for the gift of you, you have given me. I hope you meet your new son someday, but he is mine now and I shall call him Thunder."

She laughs and the others hear and laugh with her. The secret, just for them, just for fun, and we won't tell anyone.

The end, for now...

About the Author

The illustrious best-selling author and international speaker, Gary Douglas, pioneered a set of transformational life changing tools and processes known as Access Consciousness® over 20 years ago. These cutting edge tools have transformed the lives of thousands of people all over the world. In fact, his work has spread to 47 countries, with 2,000 trained facilitators worldwide. Simple but so effective, the tools facilitate people of all ages and backgrounds to help remove limitations holding them back from a full life.

Gary was born in Midwest USA and raised in San Diego, California. Although he came from a *"normal"* middle class family, he was fascinated from an early age with the human psyche and this interest grew into a desire to assist people to *"know what they know"* and expand into more awareness, joy and abundance. These pragmatic tools he has developed are not only being used by celebrities, corporates and teachers but also by health professionals (psychologists, chiropractors, naturopaths) to improve the health & wellbeing of their clients.

Prior to creating Access Consciousness® Gary Douglas was a successful realtor in Santa Barbara, California and also completed a psychology degree. Although he attained material wealth and was regarded as *"successful,"* his life began to lack meaning and so he began his search to find a new way forward- one that would create change in the world and in people's lives.

Gary is the author of 8 books including the best selling novel *"The Place."* He describes the inspiration behind the writing, *"I wanted to explore the possibilities for how life could be. To allow people to know there actually is no necessity to live with the ageing, insanity, stupidity, intrigue, violence, craziness, trauma and drama we live with, as though we have no choice. "The Place" is about people knowing that all things are possible. Choice is the source of creation. What if our choices can be changed in an instant? What if we could make choice more real than the decisions and stuck points we buy as real?"*

Gary has an incredible level of awareness and care for all living things, *"I would like people be more aware and more conscious and to realize we need to be stewards of the earth not users and abusers of the earth. If we start to see the possibilities of what we have available to us, instead of trying to create our piece of the pie, we could create a different world."*

A vibrant 70-year-old grandfather (*who is almost "ageless"*) with a very different view on life, Gary believes we are here to express our uniqueness and experience the ease and joy of living. He continues to inspire others, teaching across the world and making a massive contribution to the planet. He openly proclaims that for him, *"life is just beginning."*

Gary also has a wide range of personal and other business interests. These include: a passion for antiques (*Gary established "The Antique Guild" in Brisbane, Australia in 2012*) riding spirited stallions and breeding Costarricense De Paso horses, and an eco retreat in Costa Rica set to open in 2014.

To find out more, please visit:

www.GaryMDouglas.com
www.AccessConsciousness.com
www.Costarricense-Paso.com

Other Books By Gary M. Douglas

Talk to the Animals
Did you know that every animal, every plant, every structure on this planet has consciousness and desires to gift to you? Animals have a tremendous amount of information and amazing gifts they can give to us if we are willing to receive them.

Money Isn't The Problem, You Are
Offering out-of-the-box concepts with money. It's not about money. It never is. It's about what you're willing to receive.

Sex is Not a Four Letter Word but Relationship Often Times Is
Funny , frank, and delightfully irreverent, this book offers readers an entirely fresh view of how to create great intimacy and exceptional sex. What if you could stop guessing—and find out what REALLY works?

Magic. You Are It. Be It.
Magic is about the fun of having the things you desire. The real magic is the ability to have the joy that life can be. In this book you are presented tools & points of view that you can use to create consciousness and magic—and change your life in ways you may not even be able to imagine.

Right Riches for You!

What if generating money and having money were fun and joyful? What if, in having fun and joy with money, you receive more of it? What would that be like? Money follows joy; joy does not follow money. As seen on Lifetime Television's Balancing Act Show.

Divorceless Relationships

A Divorceless Relationship is one where you don't have to divorce any part of you in order to be in a relationship with someone else. It is a place where everyone and everything you are in a relationship with can become greater as a result of the relationship.

Lightning Source UK Ltd.
Milton Keynes UK
UKHW040755190520
363411UK00001B/14